WITHDRAWN

Swinburne Replies

Swinburne Replies

NOTES ON POEMS AND REVIEWS

UNDER THE MICROSCOPE

DEDICATORY EPISTLE

edited by
CLYDE
KENNETH
HYDER

SYRACUSE UNIVERSITY PRESS

To the memory of

CHARLES B. REALEY
(January 27, 1900—August 28, 1960)

SCHOLARLY TEACHER OF HISTORY
GENIAL AND FAITHFUL FRIEND

Preface

DURING the centenary of *Notes on Poems and Reviews* (1866), a new edition of it and of *Under the Microscope* (1872) and the *Dedicatory Epistle* (1904) seems timely. These are Swinburne's systematic replies to his critics. Containing imaginative interpretations of their author's own poems or acute criticism of other poets, as well as stimulating observations on poetry in general, they come nearer to being his *ars poetica* than anything else from his pen. Because of their relevance to a famous controversy, they occupy a strategic place in literary history. Not the least of their merits is their incorporating some of the most felicitous invective by a master of invective. Furthermore, the need for accurate texts is obvious. For many readers the first two have been accessible, if accessible at all, only in the Bonchurch Edition of Swinburne's *Collected Works,* edited by Sir Edmund Gosse and Thomas James Wise, which did not include the *Dedicatory Epistle*—perhaps, as has been suggested, because of Gosse's dislike of Theodore Watts-Dunton, to whom it was addressed. One could easily illustrate the editorial inadequacies of Gosse and Wise, painfully familiar to special students. Two small examples will suffice. The Bonchurch version of *Notes on Poems and Reviews* not only omits a quotation from the *Iliad* but incorrectly makes the following sentence begin a new paragraph. Though Swinburne listed "monsieurs" for "messieurs" among the errata, "monsieurs" turns up, incredibly, in the Bonchurch *Under the Microscope.* For these two earlier writings, *Swinburne Replies* takes account of the manuscript readings.

Only the first edition of *Notes on Poems and Reviews* has any claim to textual authority. According to Wise's *Bibliography,* the second edition, which also bears the date of 1866, is distinguishable from its predecessor by the name appearing on the reverse of the title-page, "Savill, Edwards and Co." instead of "Savill and Edwards." John Camden Hotten published it without the author's knowledge. Collation has not revealed significant differences. The

American publisher of *Poems and Ballads,* G. W. Carleton, also brought out in 1866 his own edition of *Notes,* which departed from the English text in a few minor misprints and one major misprint, near the end, according to which "the press will be as important [instead of the correct "impotent"] as the pulpit to dictate the laws and remove the landmarks of art." Though Wise's *Bibliography* ignores this edition, it does mention that in 1899 Thomas B. Mosher of Portland, Maine, published both *Notes* and *Under the Microscope,* the former with *Poems and Ballads.* The two volumes were unauthorized and so without textual value.

The manuscript of *Notes on Poems and Reviews,* in the Huntington Library, consists of twenty-nine leaves regularly numbered and nearly all full, interpolations or notes partly filling the versos of five of them. The paper is the author's favorite blue, 12 ¾ by 8 inches in size. Most of *Under the Microscope,* which is in the Harvard College Library, is on white paper of 13 by 8 inches, some leaves being smaller. The numbers at the top of the leaves run to 54 (39A, smaller in size, follows 39, but "52" is omitted, apparently by an oversight, "53" following "51"). On the back of fifteen leaves are footnotes or matter to be inserted. Someone in the printing establishments concerned has written in at intervals names of compositors responsible for setting type; otherwise both manuscripts are entirely in the poet's handwriting.

In several instances I have preferred manuscript readings, in the textual notes indicating the readings of the first edition. When readings are cited, that of the manuscript is second. Though I originally planned to include all variant readings, the large number of these involving only slight differences of punctuation led me to modify this plan. I do cite all variants that involve differences of phrasing. Special details are these: In putting quotation marks inside semicolons, not outside as in the first editions, I am following the usual order in the manuscripts. Both the first edition and the manuscript of *Notes on Poems and Reviews* use double quotation marks, though the manuscript omits them for centered lines, whereas the first edition uses both quotation marks and smaller type for such lines. Since smaller type seems sufficient unless a centered passage itself contains quoted matter, for centered lines I have omitted quotation marks without noting that the first edition includes them. The manuscript of *Under the Microscope*, instead of the double marks of *Notes*, uses single quotation marks, but I have chosen to follow the first edition rather than it (for consistency I have used double marks in the *Dedicatory Epistle*). I have also kept "show" rather than the "shew" of the manuscript. Illustrations of such details are omitted from the textual notes except as other variations in a passage may necessitate incidental recording of them. In noting manuscript readings, I have disregarded the ampersand for *and*, as well as shortened forms of words like *though*. Of course I have not tried to eliminate inconsistencies in Swinburne's use of italics and quotation marks. In his manuscripts he frequently used a semicolon where the colon of the first edition (sometimes a colon followed by a dash) seems preferable. That he chose occasionally to use a colon where recent practice favors a semicolon was partly in accordance with conventions of punctuation in his day. Though I do not depart from the readings of the first edition without manuscript authority, I see no point in not correcting misspellings, like that of *"Tannhäuser,"* even if the manuscripts contain such misspellings.

Here I may cite a few examples of superior manuscript readings. "Temptress," used in the manuscript of *Notes on Poems and Reviews,* seems preferable to "huntress," "prey" having apparently contributed to the printer's misreading. In *Under the Microscope,* "deform" could easily be mistaken for "depress," but the context favors "deform," which is certainly the word used in the manuscript. If Swinburne quoted correctly—as, for instance, a phrase of Walt Whitman's from which one may reasonably suppose the printer omitted a comma—the manuscript reading is obviously safer. Since the poet wrote of Princess Ida's "collegians," instead of the "colleagues" of the first edition (also a word of ten letters), may we not justifiably assume that we owe the substitution to the printer rather than the author? But, since there is no evidence regarding changes Swinburne could have made in proof, I have treated conservatively readings different from those of the first editions.

The textual notes at the end of this book will enable each reader to form an opinion of the author's intentions and, in doubtful cases, to make his own choice of variants. The citation of all canceled passages might reveal a little more of those intentions than does the course here pursued: in view of the disadvantages of fuller citation, I have cited only the more significant passages that are marked out but still legible. Some more extended passages in the manuscripts, deleted from the first editions, are not without autobiographical interest.

Though the quotation from the *Iliad* omitted from the text of the Bonchurch Edition may be new to most previous readers of *Notes on Poems and Reviews,* its meaning, like that of other Greek passages (including one composed by Swinburne himself), will hardly be immediately clear without editorial assistance; nor will modern readers be aware of numerous contemporary allusions. An editor cannot hope to explain every one of these or even to identify all quotations in an author so widely read and so keen of memory as Swinburne. Many of Swinburne's readers are more knowledgeable than I—though few will be more knowledgeable than he was—and may therefore consider superfluous certain explanatory notes, placed where they may be consulted or ignored, in front of the textual notes.

Nowadays students of Swinburne are under deep obligation to Professor Cecil Y. Lang of the University of Chicago, the gifted editor of *The Swinburne Letters.* I am indebted to him for sympathetic encouragement and generous assistance; nor should I omit to mention Mrs. Lang. John S. Mayfield, Curator of Manuscripts and Rare Books at the Syracuse University Library and a long-time Swinburnian, has answered queries with his wonted expertness. I have received special favors from Mr. Herbert C. Schulz, Curator, and Miss Jean Preston of the Department of Manuscripts at the Henry E. Huntington Library, Mrs. Elise Shoemaker of the Miriam Lutcher Stark Library of the University of Texas, and Dr. Eleanor L. Nicholes, Curator of the Harry Elkins Widener Collection in the Harvard College Library. The privilege of using the Newberry and the University of Chicago libraries has been rewarding. The librarians of the Watson Library of the University of Kansas again deserve my thanks, particularly those in charge of Special Collections and Interlibrary Loans. In quest of an elusive quotation from Robert Buchanan I have had bibliographical aid from Professor John A. Cassidy of Indiana University at South Bend. My friendly colleagues at the University of Kansas, Professors L. R. Lind, Harold Orel, and Austin Lashbrook, have also shown themselves helpful. For oversights that may have eluded my vigilance I am of course solely responsible.

—C. K. H.

Lawrence, Kansas
November, 1965

Contents

Introduction

Notes on Poems and Reviews answered the critics of *Poems and Ballads* (1866), a volume attacked with a bitterness rarely equaled in the annals of literary history. Charges of sensuality and immorality, sometimes of paganism and blasphemy, heavily outweighed objections on aesthetic grounds. On August 4, 1866, anonymous articles in the *Saturday Review* (by John Morley) and the *Athenaeum* (by Robert Buchanan) for different reasons condemned the book. Both reviewers were younger than Swinburne (1837–1909), Morley by more than a year and Buchanan by nearly four. One finds in their reviews traces of the youthful exuberance and intemperance, perhaps associated with the desire to impress and even to dazzle, that had led Swinburne to compose the kind of poetry they found it easy to condemn. Morley, himself sympathetic with Swinburne's political and religious heterodoxy and not without admiration for his imaginative power and metrical skill, nevertheless called the poet "the libidinous laureate of a pack of satyrs." On the other hand, Buchanan, who assailed *Poems and Ballads* with equal vigor, accused its author of insincerity, of being "unclean for the sake of uncleanness." On the same day the *London Review* pronounced it "depressing and misbegotten—in many of its constituents . . . utterly revolting," a work taking pains to shock the decencies, to revile God, to dwell on lust, bitterness, and despair.

In the days that followed, many periodicals in England and the United States placed Swinburne among the "lecherous priests of Venus," in the phrase applied to him by President Noah Porter of Yale University. The *Pall Mall Gazette* referred to "mad and miserable indecency." A whole generation, not just Morley or Buchanan, may seem to have spoken intemperately and even violently. The story, already set forth in detail, need not detain us here.[1]

[1] A book containing details, my *Swinburne's Literary Career and Fame*, originally published by the Duke University Press in 1933, was reissued in 1963 by Russell

1

After *Poems and Ballads* was withdrawn by Moxon, its publication was taken over by John Camden Hotten. Not by his own initiative but at the urging of this new publisher Swinburne answered his critics. Though he was preparing his reply as early as the first part of September, *Notes on Poems and Reviews* did not appear till the last week of October. Before completing his manuscript, the poet had discussed the strategy of his defense with his friend William Michael Rossetti, who, along with the latter's brother and William Bell Scott, like Dante Gabriel a poet-painter, saw the proofs. When W. M. Rossetti questioned Swinburne's claim for the dramatic character of certain poems, Swinburne defended his central position: "As to the antitheism of 'Félise' I know of course that *you* know that the verses represent a mood . . . not unfamiliar to me; but I must nevertheless maintain that no reader (*as* a reader) has a right (whatever he may conjecture) to assert that this is *my* faith and that the faith expressed in such things as the 'Litany' or 'Carol' ["A Christmas Carol"] or 'Dorothy' ["St. Dorothy"] is not. Of course it is a more serious expression of feeling; and of course this is evident; but it is not less formally dramatic than the others; and this is the point on which it seems necessary to insist and fair to enlarge" (*The Swinburne Letters,* ed. Cecil Y. Lang [New Haven, 1959–62], I, 193; hereafter cited as "Lang").

Swinburne was at first disinclined to accept W. M. Rossetti's suggestion that "Dolores," "The Garden of Proserpine," and "Hesperia" (three poems printed together in *Poems and Ballads;* aside from their juxtaposition, "Hesperia" mentions "my Dolores") be treated as a trilogy: "I should not like to bracket 'Dolores' and the two following as you propose. I ought (if I did) to couple with them in front harness 'The Triumph of Time' etc., as they express that state of feeling the reaction from which is expressed in 'Dolores'" (Lang, I, 197). In spite of this declaration, one should not suppose, as Lafourcade, Swinburne's French biographer, did, that the grouping was merely factitious. As just indicated, "Hesperia" itself suggests a connection with "Dolores."

---

and Russell of New York; since it was reproduced by offset, the reissue took no account of what is now known about the forgeries of T. J. Wise or the errors of Edmund Gosse.

A personal acquaintance of Swinburne's, W. H. Mallock, reports his confessing that whereas "The Triumph of Time" was "a monument to the sole real love of his life," "Dolores" had "expressed the passion with which he had sought relief, in the madnesses of the fleshly Venus, from his ruined dreams of the heavenly"; and that "The Garden of Proserpine" "expressed his revolt against the flesh and its fevers, and his longing to find a refuge from them in a haven of undisturbed rest."[2]

Later the poet recorded his amusement at the opinions of those who regarded "all the studies of passion or sensation attempted or achieved . . . as either confessions of positive fact or excursions of absolute fancy." The remark may warn us against dogmatic assumptions about the sources of Swinburne's inspiration. Of the poems in Swinburne's "trilogy," neither "The Garden of Proserpine" nor "Hesperia" was among the poems harshly criticized. *Notes* does not mention some that were, like "Les Noyades" or "The Leper." Presumably "The Leper" offended because of its coupling a dread disease with a humble and naive clerk's devotion, portrayed with subauditions of the erotic. One doubts its being intended as an outrageous assault upon contemporary sensibilities. Several details of the story—leprosy as a punishment due to God's anger, the hostility of friends and relatives, the isolation of the leprous in a hut—are details also portrayed in a medieval romance like *Amis and Amiloun,* and the poet's inspiration was mostly literary. One can hardly suppose that Swinburne had heard of some striking parallelism in the life of Alexander Latil (1816–1851), as recorded in the *Dictionary of American Biography,* which describes a woman's devotion to a husband and lover who became a poet after being afflicted with leprosy.

Swinburne did not choose to answer all objections. A general choosing his battleground may decide that a skillful attack is the best defense. He was familiar with the controversial literature of

2 *Memoirs of Life and Literature* (New York, 1920), p. 76. Incidentally, students now know, thanks to John S. Mayfield (cf. *The Victorian Poets: A Guide to Research,* ed. Frederic E. Faverty [Cambridge, Mass., 1956], p. 148), that Gosse incorrectly identified Swinburne's "sole real love"; and Cecil Y. Lang has brought to light the poet's deep attachment to the cousin who became Mrs. Disney Leith. See his "Swinburne's Lost Love," *PMLA,* LXXIV (March, 1959), 123–30.

previous literary squabbles in England and France and scornful of contemporary conventions, as indicated, for example, by such hoaxes as his pretended reviews of the imaginary authors "Félicien Cossu" and "Ernest Clouët" (now accessible in Cecil Y. Lang's *New Writings by Swinburne,* published by the Syracuse University Press in 1964). He included in his *Notes* passages interpreting certain poems and others expressing some of his deepest convictions about the poetic art. The lesson of "the fallen goddess, grown diabolic among ages that would not accept her as divine" —the goddess of "Laus Veneris"—would have been less offensive to Victorian sensibilities if some poems had not reflected their author's algolagnia, a constitutional peculiarity on which psychologists, both amateur and professional, have too abundantly dwelt. To believe that the lesson was salutary, one need not be condescending or provincial about a generation too often maligned or caricatured. A century after *Poems and Ballads* "freedom to publish" may on occasion serve to disguise literary pandering or even shield a filth industry. But Swinburne's ringing declaration still strikes home: "The question at issue is wider than any between a single writer and his critics. . . . Literature, to be worthy of men, must be large, liberal, sincere; and cannot be chaste if it be prudish."

Besides accepting most of W. M. Rossetti's advice, at the wish of his publisher Swinburne omitted a passage referring to the vague threat of prosecution (Lang, I, 199). He wanted to make the tone of his pamphlet sharp and simple, and certain phrases in his letters ("porcine hides," "the cockney pressmen") do not indicate adoption of a tactful or conciliating attitude. Not surprisingly, the immediate result was further hostility. While friends like Ruskin and Forster encouraged him, the *Examiner* (October 27, 1866), which had been friendly toward *Poems and Ballads,* was almost unique in its equally friendly reception of *Notes.* The *Pall Mall Gazette* for November 2 and the *London Review* for the following day spurned the argument that the poems are dramatic. Why, they asked, should one dramatize such subjects? The *Spectator* for November 3, which characterized *Notes* as "a very foolish and furious pamphlet . . . in which the clever, overstrong, shrieking words, though often chosen as only a poet could choose them, express nothing but weakness, white rage, studied ferocity, immeasurable thirst for vengeance," returned to the charge that *Poems and Ballads* dwells upon the morbid and the sensual. "Mr. Swinburne fastens on such subjects and feasts on them with a greedy and cruel voracity, like a famished dog at raw meat." Even *Punch* joined in the denunciation; after reading Swinburne's "defence of his prurient poetics," in its issue of November 10 it licensed the poet to change his name to "Swine-born."

II

A new volume of poems, one which both its author and modern critics have valued more highly than *Poems and Ballads,* preceded the publication of *Under the Microscope. Songs before Sunrise* (1871) brought a renewal of earlier criticism, with increasing emphasis on blasphemy and "the reddest of Red Republicanism." The *Edinburgh Review* for July, 1871, anticipates the phrasing of Robert Buchanan's notorious critique on "the fleshly school" by placing Swinburne in "the sensational school of literature" and asserting that his work derived from the corrupt French school of art and poetry.

Robert Buchanan (1841–1901) was a versatile Scottish man of letters, energetic enough to write more than fifty plays and thirty novels, besides numerous magazine articles and books of verse. Little of the verse has survived—hardly even "The Ballad of Judas Iscariot," a poem once warmly praised by such critics as George Saintsbury and Lafcadio Hearn—a poem that has roots in Buchanan's long and troubled meditations on religious questions. His rearing had fostered freethinking and heterodoxy, yet his writing reflects recurring concern with such questions. In the late sixties he was considered an important poet. George Henry Lewes and other commentators of note had praised his work and predicted for him a bright future. His contributions had appeared in leading magazines, sometimes under an assumed name. Unfortunately he was highly irascible and intemperate in his expression of opinions that were not infrequently captious. He became involved in several personal squabbles and late in life was attacking Kipling and others with the same want of moderation he had displayed in attacking D. G. Rossetti and his followers, though by that time he had come to regret and had publicly renounced what he had written of Rossetti. He was not without friends, but even they did not regard him as tactful in his personal relations.

Some events preceding Buchanan's onslaught help to explain it. Did Buchanan have a grievance against Rossetti and Swinburne? His harsh unsigned review of *Poems and Ballads* in the *Athenaeum* of August 4, 1866, has been mentioned; this had been followed by his anonymous verses in the *Spectator* of September 15, "The Session of the Poets," lampooning Swinburne. True, a letter written by Swinburne as early as January 4, 1866 (Lang, I, 146) shows that he had felt antipathy for Buchanan, being, like Doctor Johnson, anti-Scottish, but no recorded personal meeting accounts for Buchanan's hostility, and as late as January 26, 1869, Swinburne wrote Buchanan a civil note (Lang, VI, 264). But the authorship of the verses in the *Spectator* became known, accounting for W. M. Rossetti's reference, in a pamphlet defending his friend, *Swinburne's Poems and Ballads,* to the stir made by Buchanan's *London Poems*—"the advent of even so poor and pretentious a poetaster as Robert Buchanan." Buchanan expressed his resentment by the manner in which he reviewed the younger Rossetti's edition of Shelley (a work he also denounced in his pamphlet on "the fleshly school"). *A Swinburne Library* (London, 1925, p. 69) quotes a letter by Buchanan, said by Wise to have been written to Browning in March, 1872, pleading "guilty to one instinct of recrimination" and indicating his resolve "to have no mercy," because of an affront by Swinburne to the memory of David Gray, Buchanan's intimate friend and a poet of small talent whose death in 1861 had aroused sympathy, recalling the fate of John Keats. To be sure, Swinburne's reference to Gray in "Matthew Arnold's New Poems" (*Fortnightly Review,* October, 1867, not containing the footnote on Gray, added in *Essays and Studies,* 1875) seems only mildly derogatory; Swinburne had merely remarked, for those who overlooked the importance of poetic endowment, "Such talk as this of Wordsworth's is the poison of poor souls like David Gray." But an unsigned article in the *Spectator* (a magazine to which Buchanan had contributed) for October 5, 1867, after alluding to "Swinburne's incidental

sneers, like that at David Gray" (p. 1111), adds that many of
Gray's sonnets, pronounced superior to Matthew Arnold's, "will
live as long as English literature"—a remark nearly similar to
Buchanan's somewhere else: in *Under the Microscope,* having
regard to Buchanan's affectations of diction, Swinburne quoted
the Scot as prophesying that Gray would be read after other contemporaries' writings "have gone to the limbo of affettuosos."

Buchanan's article "The Fleshly School of Poetry," attributed
to "Thomas Maitland," which appeared in the *Contemporary
Review* for October, 1871, mainly assails D. G. Rossetti for his
fleshliness, singling out sonnets from *The House of Life* and a
few other poems, but denounces Swinburne for qualities he is
said to share with Rossetti, his "hysteric tone and overloaded
style." He is said to have surpassed Rossetti in blasphemy but was
"only a little mad boy letting off squibs." The pamphlet published
the following spring, *The Fleshly School of Poetry, and Other
Phenomena of the Day,* amplifies these charges, devoting more
attention to Swinburne, whose faults are rashly attributed to the
influence of Baudelaire—"the offensive choice of subject, the
obtrusion of unnatural passion, the blasphemy, the wretched ani-
malism," even the character of his women. Since he has offered
only "borrowed rubbish," Swinburne should burn his books, for-
saking such inspiration as "the smile of harlotry and the shriek of
atheism."

Reviewers of Buchanan's pamphlet were able to point to his
gross inaccuracies, the uninformed generalizations in his sopho-
moric review of English poetry, his false assumptions about "the
Italian school," and other distortions. How sincere was a book
that introduced a section called "Pearls from the Amatory Poets"?
Few intelligent readers could now overlook the lapses of taste.

The *Athenaeum* for May 25, 1872, in particular recalled the
compromising circumstances in which Buchanan's *Contemporary
Review* article had appeared. In his reply to Buchanan, "The
Stealthy School of Criticism," D. G. Rossetti, besides citing examples of quotations that were unfair or out of context, made telling
use of Buchanan's having hidden his identity under the pseudonym "Thomas Maitland." Along with Rossetti's reply, in the
Athenaeum for December 16, 1871, appeared two other letters.

One, from Strahan and Company (publishers of the *Contemporary Review*), in response to the *Athenaeum*'s having on December 2 identified "Thomas Maitland" as Robert Buchanan, asserted that to attribute the article to him was no more justifiable than to attribute it to Browning, Lytton, "or any other Robert." The other, from Buchanan, admitted the authorship of the article, alleging that his name had been suppressed by "an inadvertence," as the publisher of the *Contemporary Review* could testify. On December 30 appeared another letter by Buchanan, referring to Strahan's assuming responsibility for the pseudonym and claiming that it had been affixed when he himself was out of reach, "cruising on the shores of the western Hebrides." Statements by publisher and author were not in accord, nor was Buchanan's first statement in agreement with what he says in the preface to his pamphlet, that his essay had been signed "Thomas Maitland" so that "the criticism might rest upon its own merits and gain nothing from the name of the real writer." If Buchanan had ever intended to sign it, how may one explain the references in the article to his own poetry (one recalls, too, the mention of himself among the poets in his anonymous verses of 1866, "The Session of the Poets")? "Thomas Maitland" as a pseudonym for Buchanan must have occurred to someone familiar with the association of the name with the sixteenth-century Latinist George Buchanan (cf. page 83 note, below). Who is more likely to have thought of that association than Robert Buchanan himself?

Next to Buchanan, the critic who gets most attention in *Under the Microscope* is Alfred Austin—"sickly, broken-winded Austin," as Swinburne calls him in some verses apparently written soon after the attacks on *Poems and Ballads* (*The Ashley Library*, VI, 187). In 1869 the poet could see "no varying degrees of imbecility and insolence in the Austin creature's literary evacuations" (Lang, II, 46). Ahead of Austin was a future no kinder than Buchanan's, since he lived to be poet laureate—a post Buchanan also wanted; both men, mindful of their ambition, made gestures aimed at currying favor with Tennyson. Since Austin had the advantage of knowing Lord Salisbury, after Tennyson's death it was he who obtained the appointment. According to his biographer, Norton B. Crowell, as poet laureate Austin was a favorite subject of levity and an object of derision both at social gatherings and in *Punch*'s satiric sallies. Protected by the armor of a conceit more impenetrable than coats of mail, to all this he was indifferent.

This humorless poet, notorious for the most prosaic lines written in the nineteenth century, issued in 1870 his *Poetry of . the Period,* based largely on magazine articles previously appearing in *Temple Bar.* His leading idea was that the age was not capable of producing great poetry, and he compares Tennyson, Browning, and Swinburne unfavorably with Byron, the poet he most admired; in reply, Browning alluded to him as "Banjo-Byron."

Discussion of Byron had been stimulated by the publication of Harriet Beecher Stowe's sensational article, in September, 1869, "The True Story of Lady Byron's Life," in *Macmillan's Magazine* and in the *Atlantic Monthly.* Austin himself, among others, had answered it. (Readers who feel more sympathetic to Mrs. Stowe than either Austin or Swinburne did should remind themselves that even in the light of evidence available only in recent times differences of opinion exist.) Swinburne's analysis of Byron's assets and liabilities, in *Under the Microscope,* seems sound. The critics' comparison of Byron with Tennyson (Abraham Hayward in the *Quarterly Review* for October, 1871, had, like Austin, made the comparison) led Swinburne to defend Tennyson's superiority as a lyric poet. His own artistic conservatism, his belief that Tennyson's treatment had robbed some of the old stories of their earlier strength and dignity, led him to denounce certain aspects of *The Idylls of the King* so vigorously that one passage had to be replaced by means of a cancel. The leaf that contained the reading of the manuscript ("that cycle of strumpets and scoundrels, broken by here and there an imbecile") was removed, the substituted leaf reading "that cycle of more or less symbolic agents and patients."[3]

In his *Poetry of the Period* Alfred Austin also disparaged Walt Whitman. Swinburne was among the early Whitman en-

[3] In *A Swinburne Library* (pp. 64–65), Wise quotes a letter from a former employee of David White, who was called by Swinburne "the nominal publisher" (publication was arranged by F. S. Ellis), in regard to the removal of the canceled leaf and its replacement.

thusiasts in England, though his critical comments were more judicious than those of W. M. Rossetti, whose faithful labors in Whitman's behalf accomplished much for the poet's reputation overseas, a high point being his *Poems by Walt Whitman* (1868). Robert Buchanan, too, was an important champion, one of his letters in behalf of Whitman exciting even Austin's sympathy.[4]

Swinburne liked to maintain that *Under the Microscope* was a critical discussion of "the relative excellencies and short comings of Lord Byron and Mr. Tennyson as poets, and the respective merits and demerits of the first poet of American democracy" (Lang, III, 27). This explanation was natural for Swinburne not only because he was interested in the literary question but also because of his reluctance to seem to answer criticism of himself, as illustrated by the attitude expressed in *Notes on Poems and Reviews*. A passage in that work anticipates his pretending to devote himself to the science of comparative entomology. He first considers the insect "anonym," one of its kind being the author of a *Quarterly Review* article, Abraham Hayward. Swinburne then glances briefly at the "coprophagi," insects subsisting on uncleanness. Though Swinburne scorns to mention names of these, he could have had in mind, among others, Mortimer Collins, whose novel *Two Plunges for a Pearl* (1871) introduces Reginald Swynfen, obviously a defamatory caricature of the poet. Swinburne then passes to the comparison of Tennyson and Byron, whom Austin had exalted at the expense of modern poets; these Austin had accused of effeminacy. Having defended Tennyson's best work, Swinburne censures his treatment of the Arthurian legend. His criticism of Whitman, the subject of the fine poetic tribute that had already appeared in *Songs before Sunrise,* contains some judicious reservations, from which the later harsh comments in "Whitmania," to be written after many years of hearing Whitman praised injudiciously, naturally evolved. Buchanan himself is the target of the final broadside: to have discharged much irony and direct excoriation at him earlier might have seemed to magnify his importance. The story of Buchanan's feeble retort and of the involvements leading to his lawsuit against the *Examiner* in

---

[4] Harold Blodgett, *Walt Whitman in England* (Ithaca, New York, 1934), p. 81.

1876, because of its publishing Swinburne's letter "The Devil's Due," will not be repeated here.

In *Under the Microscope* Swinburne was as usual a stimulating critic, more perceptive than most of his contemporaries. Of course only a staunch Swinburnian could unreservedly praise the vigor of his prose style. (Even a Swinburnian may mildly demur to the length of a paragraph filling twenty-seven pages in *Under the Microscope;* it may seem long, but the result is not mere breathlessness.) The faithful Swinburnian enjoys encountering elsewhere in the poet's writings little gems of invective, as when the poet mentions "the chattering duncery and the impudent malignity of so consummate and pseudosophical a quack as George Henry Lewes" (Bonchurch Edition, XIV, 77), or learns that Lewes' consort, George Eliot, struck Swinburne as "the pitiful and unseemly spectacle of an Amazon thrown sprawling over the crupper of her spavined and spur-galled Pegasus" (*ibid.*, XIV, 12). One is not surprised, therefore, that Mrs. Stowe appears in *Under the Microscope* as "a blatant bassarid of Boston, a rampant Maenad of Massachusetts" or "a plume-plucked Celaeno." Though such phrases may sometimes seem undeserved, they were usually not unprovoked. This admiring student of Rabelais and Carlyle could hail the latter as "St. Thomas of Coprostom, late of Craigenputtock and Chelsea" (*ibid.*, XIII, 137)—the retort discourteous not only combining "copro-" and "Tom," with perhaps a glance at "Teufelsdröckh" (or "Devilsdung") but also at "Chrysostom," the Greek church father. But Carlyle had been quoted, apparently by Emerson, as comparing Swinburne to a man standing in a cesspool. As for Emerson himself, it was only after he was reported, accurately or inaccurately, to have called Swinburne "a perfect leper" that he became "a gap-toothed and hoary-headed ape, carried first into notice on the shoulder of Carlyle, . . . who now, in his dotage, spits and chatters from a dirtier perch of his own finding and fouling" (Lang, II, 274).

Under the Microscope contains Swinburne's most masterly denigration of an author by turning his own words against him, so that in the end "landsman and seaman, Londoner and Scotchman, Delian and Patarene Buchanan" is stripped of ordinary human dignity and left with the serpent that creeps and crawls, the very prototype of original sin. Presumably one may appreciate "Delian and Patarene Buchanan" better if one catches the echo of Horace's *"Delius et Patareus Apollo"* for "the god of song," but only Buchanan's own self-revelations could barb a statement like ". . . the god of song himself had not more names or addresses."

But are all the quotations what they profess to be? In a passage near the beginning Swinburne quotes a stanza in ottava rima, not yet found in older poets known to have used that meter, and a passage in the same vein said to be by a French poet. (See illustration, p. 41.) Like much of Swinburne's French verse, the lines remind one of Hugo, but an assiduous search in Hugo and other French poets has had only negative results. Probably not by mere coincidence the passage contains phrases and rhymes reminiscent of Hugo that also appear in Swinburne's literary hoax *Félicien Cossu.* The hypothesis that Swinburne himself composed it finds strongest support in the manuscript of *Under the Microscope:* the existence of changes and canceled passages is explicable only if we are seeing the poet in the act of composition, not merely in the act of recalling. The reader may not need to be reminded of the French prose that Swinburne composed to accompany "Laus Veneris" and "The Leper" or of the supposititious French critic that he introduced in his essay on Matthew Arnold's poems.

A study of the strategy of *Under the Microscope* increases one's respect for its author's literary resources and his skill in using them. Adapting some lines from Euripides or Shakespeare, quoting from Aeschylus or Landor, or introducing a mythological allusion like that of Hercules' thirteenth labor—these are in themselves slight as a feather, but a feather which this fletcher deftly fits to an arrow aimed at a vulnerable spot in his foes' armor. Though a modern commentator writes of Swinburne's irony as "heavy," "weighty" seems more just for this masterpiece of sustained irony.

Appreciation of it is overdue, for Swinburne's contemporaries largely ignored it. The *Examiner* for July 6, 1872, published a somewhat deprecating notice. The poet mentions "the concerted silence of literary London" (Lang, II, 200). He observed that even those who had promised to review the volume failed to do so. He came to wish that he had published it in an essay in the *Fortnightly Review* rather than as a pamphlet (*ibid.*, II, 252), and he toyed with the idea of including both it and *Notes* in his *Essays and Studies* (*ibid.*, II, 242, 252). On May 9, 1877, writing of its critical fate, he stated that "its one edition was rapidly exhausted—a second was not called for" and that "the main thing memorable," which afforded him "inexpressible amusement," was its being listed "in a published German catalogue of the year's scientific publications throughout Europe" (*ibid.*, IV, 2).

III

Notes on Poems and Reviews discussed some of his early poems as only a poet could. In *Under the Microscope* Swinburne launched a counterattack against the critics of D. G. Rossetti and himself. The third of his ambitious replies, the *Dedicatory Epistle* to the Collected Poems (1904), answered a few particular and some more general criticisms. As early as July 27, 1896, he had formulated plans for it (*ibid.*, VI, 105). A month later he had written "a page or so" (p. 110), and some days afterward he expressed the resolve to "get the business off my hands once for all as soon as may be. I could not think of having to take up the task again" (p. 113). We do not know when this "prefatory essay in auto-criticism," as he called it in 1904 (*ibid.*, VI, 184), was finished. An introductory sentence mentions "thirty-six years" after the publication of *Poems and Ballads* (the American edition of 1905 reads "thirty-eight"); this would seem to imply the completion of the essay by 1902. Even earlier it may have been nearly complete.

In writing it, Swinburne remembered the applause of Sir Henry Taylor and of Victor Hugo. He affirmed that, though the esteem of Mazzini had been precious, his attitude towards Mazzini or Hugo had not been that of an idolator. He recalled particular comments—for instance, that the philosophic musings in *Tristram of Lyonesse* are anachronistic. Some criticism of his plays had been misguided; he averred that he had written for the Globe or the Red Bull, not for the contemporary theater.

Among the recurring criticisms of Swinburne during his later years, two stand out. One was the charge of bookishness. Hence he sturdily maintains that books are valid sources of inspiration, whatever they may be to "the half-brained creature to whom books are other than living things." To the second complaint, that his verse eclipses or sacrifices thought, Swinburne's answer is less simple, though on the surface similar: "Except to such ears as should always be kept closed against poetry, there is no music in verse which has not in it sufficient fullness and ripeness of meaning, sufficient adequacy of emotion or of thought, to abide the analysis of any other than the blind scrutiny of prepossession or the squint-eyed inspection of malignity." These words are weighted with the consciousness of hostility from a generation of critics, who are told that they cannot see clearly. Poets can. Swinburne is here affirming what he had already said in *Under the Microscope* and in other places: ". . . wherever you catch a note of good music you will surely find that it came whence only it could come, from some true root of music in the thought or thing spoken" (below, p. 65). In "The Hero as Poet," Carlyle, too, had stated: "A *musical* thought is one spoken by a mind that has penetrated into the inmost heart of the thing; detected the inmost mystery of it, namely the *melody* that lies hidden in it; the inward harmony of coherence which is its soul." To Swinburne poetry was not music capable of separation from thought; it was more than the sum of two theoretical components, being something organic. The inner harmony of verse is related to the poet's interpretation of nature, a harmony springing out of wholeness of vision. Will anyone who has heard "The Garden of Proserpine" or the choruses from *Atalanta*, for example, read with sensitivity to meaning—that is, to both melody and thought— worry about the criticism?

NOTES ON POEMS
AND REVIEWS

NOTES ON POEMS AND REVIEWS

NOTES ON POEMS AND REVIEWS

BY

ALGERNON CHARLES SWINBURNE.

" Je pense sur ces satires comme Épictète : 'Si l'on dit du mal de toi, et qu'il soit véritable, corrige-toi ; si ce sont des mensonges, ris-en.' J'ai appris avec l'âge à devenir bon cheval de poste ; je fais ma station, et ne m'embarrasse pas des roquets qui aboient en chemin."—*Frédéric le Grand*.

" Ignorance by herself is an awkward lumpish wench ; not yet fallen into vicious courses, nor to be uncharitably treated : but Ignorance and Insolence, these are, for certain, an unlovely Mother and Bastard !"—*Carlyle*.

LONDON :

JOHN CAMDEN HOTTEN, PICCADILLY.

1866.

IT is by no wish of my own that I accept the task now proposed to me. To vindicate or defend myself from the assault or the charge of men whom, but for their attacks, I might never have heard of, is an office which I, or any writer who respects his work, cannot without reluctance stoop to undertake. As long as the attacks[1] on my book—I have seen a few, I am told there are many —were confined within the usual limits[2] of the anonymous press, I let them pass without the notice to which they appeared to aspire. Sincere or insincere, insolent or respectful, I let my assailants say out their say unheeded.[3]

I have now undertaken to write a few words on this affair, not by way of apology or vindication, of answer or appeal. I have none such to offer. Much of the criticism I have seen is as usual, in the words of Shakspeare's greatest follower,

> As if a man should spit against the wind;
> The filth returns in's face.[4]

In recognition of his fair dealing with me in this matter, I am bound by my own sense of right to accede to the wish of my present publisher,[5] and to the wishes of friends whose advice I value, that on his account, if not on mine, I should make some reply to the charges brought against me—as far as I understand them. The work is not fruitful of pleasure, of honour, or of profit; but, like other such tasks, it may be none the less useful and necessary. I am aware that it cannot be accomplished without some show of egotism; and I am perforce prepared to incur the consequent charge of arrogance. The office of commentator on my own works has been forced upon me by circumstances connected with the issue and re-issue of my last book.[6] I am compelled to look sharply into it, and inquire what passage, what allusion, or what phrase can have drawn down such sudden thunder from the serene heavens of public virtue.[7] A mere libeller I have no wish to encounter; I leave it to saints to fight with beasts at Ephesus or nearer. "For in these strifes, and on such persons, it were as wretched to affect a victory, as it is unhappy to be committed with them."

Certain poems of mine, it appears, have been impugned by judges,[8] with or without a name, as indecent or as blasphemous.[9] To me, as I have intimated, their verdict is a matter of infinite indifference: it is of equally small moment to me whether in such eyes as theirs I appear moral or immoral, Christian or pagan. But, remembering that science must not scorn to investigate animalcules and infusoria, I am ready for once to play the anatomist.

With regard to any opinion implied or expressed throughout my book, I desire that one thing should be remembered: the book is dramatic, many-faced, multifarious; and no utterance of enjoyment or despair, belief or unbelief, can properly be assumed as the assertion of its author's personal feeling or faith. Were each poem to be accepted as the deliberate outcome and result of the writer's conviction, not mine alone but most other men's verses would leave nothing behind them but a sense of cloudy chaos and suicidal contradiction. Byron and Shelley, speaking in their own persons, and with what sublime effect we know, openly and insultingly mocked and reviled what the English of their day held most sacred. I have not done this. I do not say that, if I chose, I would not do so to the best of my power; I do say that hitherto I have seen fit to do nothing of the kind.[10]

It remains then to inquire what in that book can be reasonably offensive to the English reader. In order to resolve this problem, I will not fish up any of the ephemeral scurrilities born only to sting if they can, and sink as they must. I will take the one article that lies before me; the work (I admit) of an enemy, but the work (I acknowledge) of a gentleman. I cannot accept it as accurate; but I readily and gladly allow that it neither contains nor suggests anything false or filthy. To him therefore, rather than to another, I address my reclamation. Two among my poems, it appears, are in his opinion "especially horrible." Good. Though the phrase be somewhat "inexpressive," I am content to meet him on this ground. It is something—nay, it is much—to find an antagonist who has a sufficient sense of honesty and honour to

mark out the lists in which he, the challenger, is desirous to encounter the challenged.

The first, it appears, of these especially horrible poems is
Anactoria. I am informed, and have not cared to verify the assertion, that this poem has excited, among the chaste and candid
critics of the day or hour or minute, a more vehement reprobation,
a more virtuous horror, a more passionate appeal, than any other
of my writing. Proud and glad as I must be of this distinction, I
must yet, however reluctantly, inquire what merit or demerit has
incurred such unexpected honour.[11] I was not ambitious of it; I
am not ashamed of it; but I am overcome by it. I have never
lusted[12] after the praise of reviewers; I have never feared their
abuse; but I would fain know why the vultures should gather here
of all places; what congenial carrion they smell, who can discern
such (it is alleged) in any rose-bed. And after a little reflection
I do know, or conjecture. Virtue, as she appears incarnate in
British journalism and voluble through that unsavoury organ, is
something of a compound creature—

> A lump neither alive nor dead,
> Dog-headed, bosom-eyed, and bird-footed;

nor have any dragon's jaws been known to emit on occasion
stronger and stranger sounds and odours. But having, not without astonishment and disgust, inhaled these odours, I find myself
at last able to analyse their component parts. What my poem
means, if any reader should want that explained, I am ready to
explain, though perplexed by the hint that explanation may be
required. What certain reviewers have imagined it to imply, I am
incompetent to explain, and unwilling to imagine. I am evidently
not virtuous enough to understand them. I thank Heaven that I
am not. *Ma corruption rougirait de leur pudeur.* I have not studied
in those schools whence that full-fledged phœnix, the "virtue" of
professional pressmen, rises chuckling and crowing from the
dunghill, its birthplace and its deathbed. But there are birds of
alien feather, if not of higher flight; and these I would now recall
into no hencoop or preserve of mine, but into the open and general field where all may find pasture and sunshine and fresh air:
into places whither the prurient prudery and the virulent virtue

of pressmen and prostitutes cannot follow; into an atmosphere where calumny cannot speak, and fatuity cannot breathe; in a word, where backbiters and imbeciles become impossible. I neither hope nor wish to change the unchangeable, to purify the impure. To conciliate them, to vindicate myself in their eyes, is a task which I should not condescend to attempt, even were I sure to accomplish.[13]

In this poem I have simply expressed, or tried to express, that violence of affection between one and another which hardens into rage and deepens into despair. The key-note which I have here touched was struck long since by Sappho. We in England are taught, are compelled under penalties to learn, to construe, and to repeat, as schoolboys, the imperishable and incomparable verses of that supreme poet; and I at least am grateful for the training. I have wished, and I have even ventured to hope, that I might be in time competent to translate into a baser and later language the divine words which even when a boy I could not but recognise as divine. That hope, if indeed I dared ever entertain such a hope, I soon found fallacious. To translate the two odes and the remaining fragments of Sappho is the one impossible task; and as witness of this I will call up one of the greatest among poets. Catullus "translated"—or as his countrymen would now say "traduced"— the Ode to Anactoria—Εἰς Ἐρωμέναν: a more beautiful translation there never was and will never be; but compared with the Greek, it is colourless and bloodless, puffed out by additions and enfeebled by alterations. Let any one set against each other the two first stanzas, Latin and Greek, and pronounce. (This would be too much to ask of all of my critics; but some among the journalists of England may be capable of achieving the not exorbitant task.) Where Catullus failed I could not hope to succeed; I tried instead to reproduce in a diluted and dilated form the spirit of a poem which could not be reproduced in the body.

Now, the ode Εἰς Ἐρωμέναν—the "Ode to Anactoria" (as it is named by tradition)—the poem which English boys have to get by heart—the poem (and this is more important) which has in the whole world of verse no companion and no rival but the Ode to Aphrodite, has been twice at least translated or "traduced." I am not aware that Mr. Ambrose Phillips, or M. Nicolas Boileau-

Despréaux, was ever impeached before any jury of moralists for his sufficiently grievous offence. By any jury of poets both[14] would assuredly have been convicted. Now, what they did I have not done. To the best (and bad is the best) of their ability, they have "done into" bad French and bad English the very words of Sappho. Feeling that although I might do it better I could not do it well, I abandoned the idea of translation—ἔχων ἀέχοντί γε θυμῷ. I tried, then, to write some paraphrase of the fragment which the Fates and the Christians have spared us. I have not said, as Boileau and Phillips have, that the speaker sweats and swoons at sight of her favourite by the side[15] of a man. I have abstained from touching on such details, for this reason: that I felt myself incompetent to give adequate expression in English to the literal and absolute words of Sappho; and would not debase and degrade them into a viler form. No one can feel more deeply than I do the inadequacy of my work. "That is not Sappho," a friend said once to me. I could only reply, "It is as near as I can come; and no man can come close to her." Her remaining verses are the supreme success, the final achievement, of the poetic art.

But this, it may be, is not to the point. I will try to draw thither; though the descent is immeasurable from Sappho's verse to mine, or to any man's. I have striven to cast my spirit into the mould of hers, to express and represent not the poem but the poet. I did not think it requisite to disfigure the page with a foot-note wherever I had fallen back upon the original text. Here and there, I need not say, I have rendered into English the very words of Sappho. I have tried also to work into words of my own some expression of their effect: to bear witness how, more than any other's, her verses strike and sting the memory in lonely places, or at sea, among all loftier sights and sounds—how they seem akin to fire and air, being themselves "all air and fire"; other element there is none in them. As to the angry appeal against the supreme mystery of oppressive heaven, which I have ventured to put into her mouth at that point only where pleasure culminates in pain, affection in anger, and desire in despair—as to the "blasphemies"* against God or Gods of which here and elsewhere I stand

---

* As I shall not return to this charge of "blasphemy," I will here cite a notable instance of what does seem permissible in that line to the English reader. (I need

accused,—they are to be taken as the first outcome or outburst of foiled and fruitless passion recoiling on itself. After this, the spirit finds time to breathe and repose above all vexed senses of the weary body, all bitter labours of the revolted soul; the poet's pride of place is resumed, the lofty conscience of invincible immortality in the memories and the mouths of men.

What is there now of horrible in this? the expressions of fierce fondness, the ardours of passionate despair? Are these so unnatural as to affright or disgust? Where is there an unclean detail? where an obscene allusion? A writer as impure as my critics might of course have written, on this or on any subject, an impure poem; I have not. And if[16] to translate or paraphrase Sappho be an offence,[17] indict the heavier offenders who have handled and rehandled this matter in their wretched versions of the ode. Is my poem more passionate in detail, more unmistakable in subject? I affirm that it is less; and what I affirm I have proved.

Next on the list of accusation stands the poem of *Dolores*. The gist and bearing of this I should have thought evident enough, viewed by the light of others which precede and follow it. I have striven here[19] to express that transient state of spirit through which a man may be supposed to pass, foiled in love and weary of loving, but not yet in sight of rest; seeking refuge in those "violent delights" which "have violent ends," in fierce and frank sensualities which at least profess to be no more than they are. This poem, like *Faustine*, is so distinctly symbolic and fanciful that it cannot justly be amenable to judgment as a study in the school of realism. The spirit, bowed and discoloured by suffering and by passion (which are indeed the same thing and the same

---

not say that I do not question the right, which hypocrisy and servility would deny, of author and publisher to express and produce what they please. I do not deprecate, but demand for all men freedom to speak and freedom to hear. It is the line of demarcation which admits, if offence there be, the greater offender and rejects the less—it is this that I do not understand.) After many alternate curses and denials of God, a great poet talks of Christ "veiling his horrible Godhead," of his "malignant soul," his "godlike malice." Shelley outlived all this and much more; but Shelley wrote all this and much more. Will no Society for the Suppression of Common Sense—no Committee for the Propagation of Cant—see to it a little? or have they not already tried their hands at it and broken down? For the poem which contains the words above quoted continues at this day to bring credit and profit to its publishers—Messrs. Moxon and Co.[18]

word), plays for a while[20] with its pleasures and its pains, mixes and distorts them with a sense half-humorous and half-mournful, exults in bitter and doubtful emotions—[21]

Moods of fantastic sadness, nothing worth.

It sports with sorrow, and jests against itself; cries out for freedom and confesses the chain; decorates with the name of goddess, crowns anew as the mystical Cotytto, some woman, real or ideal, in whom the pride of life with its companion lusts is incarnate. In her lover's half-shut eyes, her fierce unchaste beauty is transfigured, her cruel sensual eyes have a meaning and a message; there are memories and secrets in the kisses of her lips. She is the darker Venus, fed with burnt-offering and blood-sacrifice; the veiled image of that pleasure which men impelled by satiety and perverted by power have sought through ways as strange as Nero's before and since his time; the daughter of lust and death, and holding of both her parents; Our Lady of Pain, antagonist alike of trivial sins and virtues; no Virgin, and unblessed of men; no mother of the Gods or God; no Cybele, served by sexless priests or monks, adored of Origen or of Atys; no likeness of her in Dindymus or Loreto.

The next act in this lyrical monodrama of passion represents a new stage and scene. The worship of desire has ceased; the mad commotion of sense has stormed itself out; the spirit,[22] clear of the old regret that drove it upon such violent ways for a respite, healed of the fever that wasted it in the search for relief among fierce fancies and tempestuous pleasures, dreams now of truth discovered and repose attained. Not the martyr's ardour of selfless love, an unprofitable flame that burnt out and did no service—not the rapid rage of pleasure that seemed for a little to make the flesh divine, to clothe the naked senses with the fiery raiment of faith; but a stingless love, an innocuous desire. "Hesperia," the tenderest type of woman or of dream, born in the westward "islands of the blest," where the shadows of all happy and holy things live beyond the sunset a sacred and a sleepless life, dawns upon his eyes a western dawn, risen as the fiery day of passion goes down, and risen where it sank. Here, between moonrise and sunset, lives the love that is gentle and faithful, neither giving too much nor asking—a bride rather than a mistress, a sister rather than a bride. But not at once, or not for ever, can the past be killed and buried; hither also the temptress[23] follows her flying prey, wounded and weakened, still fresh from the fangs of passion; the cruel hands, the amorous eyes, still glitter and allure. *Qui a bu boira:* the feet are drawn back towards the ancient ways. Only by lifelong flight, side by side with the goddess that redeems, shall her slave of old escape from the goddess that consumes: if even thus one may be saved, even thus distance the bloodhounds.

This is the myth or fable of my poem; and it is not without design that I have slipped in, between the first and the second part, the verses called *The Garden of Proserpine,* expressive, as I meant they should be, of that brief total pause of passion and of thought, when the spirit, without fear or hope of good things or evil, hungers and thirsts only after the perfect sleep. Now, what there is in all this unfit to be written—what there is here indecent in manner or repulsive in matter—I at least do not yet see; and before I can see it, my eyes must be purged with the euphrasy and rue which keep clear the purer eyes of professional virtue. The insight into evil of chaste and critical pressmen, their sharp scent for possible or impossible impurities, their delicate ear for a sound or a whisper of wrong—all this knowledge "is too wonderful and excellent for me; I cannot attain unto it." In one thing, indeed, it seems I have erred: I have forgotten to prefix to my work the timely warning of a great poet and humorist:—

> J'en préviens les mères des familles,
> Ce que j'écris n'est pas pour les petites filles
> Dont on coupe le pain en tartines; mes vers
> Sont des vers de jeune homme.

I have overlooked the evidence which every day makes clearer, that our time has room only for such as are content to write for children and girls. But this oversight is the sum of my offence.

It would seem indeed as though to publish a book were equivalent to thrusting it with violence into the hands of every mother and nurse in the kingdom as fit and necessary food for female infancy. Happily there is no fear that the supply of milk for babes will fall short of the demand for some time yet. There are moral milkmen enough, in all conscience, crying their ware about the streets and by-ways; fresh or stale, sour or sweet, the requisite fluid runs from a sufficiently copious issue. In due time, perhaps, the critical doctors may prescribe a stronger diet for their hypochondriac patient, the reading world; or that gigantic *malade imaginaire* called the public may rebel against the weekly draught or the daily drug of MM. Purgon and Diafoirus. We, meanwhile, who profess to deal neither in poison nor in pap, may not unwillingly stand aside. Let those read who will, and let those who will abstain from reading. *Caveat emptor.* No one wishes to force men's food down the throats of babes and sucklings. The verses last analysed were assuredly written with no moral or immoral design; but the upshot seems to me moral rather than immoral, if it must needs be one or the other, and if (which I cannot be sure of) I construe aright those somewhat misty and changeable terms.

These poems thus disposed of are (I am told) those which have given most offence and scandal to the venal virtue of journalism. As I have not to review my reviewers, I need not be at pains to refute at length every wilful error or unconscious lie which a workman that way inclined might drag into light. To me, as to all others who may read what I write, the whole matter must continue to seem too pitiable and trivial to waste a word or thought on it which we can help wasting. But having begun this task, I will add yet a word or two of annotation. I have heard that even the little poem of *Faustine* has been to some readers a thing to make the scalp creep and the blood freeze. It was issued with no such intent. Nor do I remember that any man's voice or heel was lifted against it when it first appeared, a new-born and virgin poem, in the *Spectator* newspaper for 1862. Virtue, it would seem, has shot up surprisingly in the space of four years or less—a rank and rapid growth, barren of blossom and rotten at root. *Faustine* is the reverie of a man gazing on the bitter and vicious loveliness of a face as common and as cheap as the morality of reviewers, and dreaming of past lives in which this fair face may have held a nobler or fitter station; the imperial profile may have been Faustina's, the thirsty lips a Mænad's, when first she learnt to drink blood or wine, to waste the loves and ruin the lives of men;

through Greece and again through Rome she may have passed with the same face which now comes before us dishonoured and discrowned. Whatever of merit or demerit there may be in the verses, the idea that gives them such life as they have is simple enough:[24] the transmigration of a single soul, doomed as though by accident from the first to all evil and no good, through many ages and forms, but clad always in the same type of fleshly beauty. The chance which suggested to me this poem was one which may happen any day to any man—the sudden sight of a living face which recalled the well-known likeness of another dead for centuries: in this instance, the noble and faultless type of the elder Faustina, as seen in coin and bust. Out of that casual glimpse and sudden recollection these verses sprang and grew.

Of the poem in which I have attempted once more to embody the legend of Venus and her knight, I need say only that my first aim was to rehandle the old story in a new fashion. To me it seemed that the tragedy began with the knight's return to Venus —began at the point where hitherto it had seemed to leave off. The immortal agony of a man lost after all repentance—cast down from fearful hope into fearless despair—believing in Christ and bound to Venus—desirous of penitential pain, and damned to joyless pleasure—this, in my eyes, was the kernel and nucleus of a myth comparable only to that of the foolish virgins, and bearing the same burden. The tragic touch of the story is this: that the knight who has renounced Christ believes in him; the lover who has embraced Venus disbelieves in her. Vainly and in despair would he make the best of that which is the worst—vainly remonstrate with God, and argue on the side he would fain desert. Once accept or admit the least admixture of pagan worship, or of modern thought, and the whole story collapses into froth and smoke. It was not till my poem was completed that I received from the hands of its author the admirable pamphlet of Charles Baudelaire on Wagner's *Tannhäuser*.[25] If any one desires to see, expressed in better words than I can command, the conception of the mediæval Venus which it was my aim to put into verse, let him turn to the magnificent passage in which M. Baudelaire describes the fallen goddess, grown diabolic among ages that would not accept her as divine. In another point, as I then found,

I concur with the great musician and his great panegyrist. I have made Venus the one love of her knight's whole life, as Mary Stuart of Chastelard's; I have sent him, poet and soldier, fresh to her fierce embrace. Thus only both legend and symbol appear to me noble and significant. Light loves and harmless errors must not touch the elect of heaven or of hell. The queen of evil, the lady of lust, will endure no rival but God; and when the vicar of God rejects him, to her only can he return to abide the day of his judgment in weariness and sorrow and fear.

These poems do not seem to me condemnable, unless it be on the ground of bad verse; and to any charge of that kind I should of course be as unable as reluctant to reply. But I certainly was even less prepared to hear the batteries of virtue open fire in another quarter. Sculpture I knew was a dead art,[26] buried centuries deep out of sight, with no angel keeping watch over the sepulchre; its very grave-clothes divided by wrangling and impotent sectaries, and no chance anywhere visible of a resurrection. I knew that belief in the body was the secret of sculpture, and that a past age of ascetics could no more attempt or attain it than the present age of hypocrites; I knew that modern moralities and recent religions were, if possible, more averse and alien to this purely physical and pagan art than to the others; but how far averse I did not know. There is nothing lovelier, as there is nothing more famous, in later Hellenic art, than the statue of Hermaphroditus. No one would compare it with the greatest works of Greek sculpture. No one would lift Keats on a level with Shakespeare. But the Fates have allowed us to possess at once Othello and Hyperion, Theseus and Hermaphroditus. At Paris, at Florence, at Naples, the delicate divinity of this work has always drawn towards it the eyes of artists and poets.* A creature at

---

* Witness Shelley's version:—

> "A sexless thing it was, and in its growth
> It seemed to have developed no defect
> Of either sex, yet all the grace of both;
> In gentleness and strength its limbs were decked;
> The bosom lightly swelled with its full youth,
> The countenance was such as might select
> Some artist, that his skill should never die,
> Imaging forth such perfect purity."
>
> *Witch of Atlas*, st. xxxvi.

once foul and dull enough to extract from a sight so lovely, from a thing so noble, the faintest, the most fleeting idea of impurity, must be, and must remain, below comprehension and below remark. It is incredible that the meanest of men should derive from it any other than the sense of high and grateful pleasure. Odour and colour and music are not more tender or more pure. How favourite and frequent a vision among the Greeks was this of the union of sexes in one body of perfect beauty, none need be told. In Plato the legend has fallen into a form coarse, hard, and absurd. The theory of God splitting in two the double archetype of man and woman, the original hermaphrodite which had to get itself bisected into female and male, is repulsive and ridiculous enough. But the idea thus incarnate, literal or symbolic, is merely beautiful. I am not the first who has translated into written verse this sculptured poem: another before me, as he says, has more than once "caressed it with a sculptor's love." It is, indeed, among statues as a lyric among tragedies; it stands below the Niobe as Simonides below Æschylus, as Correggio beneath Titian. The sad and subtle moral of this myth, which I have desired to indicate in verse, is that perfection once attained on all sides is a thing thenceforward barren of use or fruit; whereas the divided beauty of separate woman and man—a thing inferior and imperfect— can serve all turns of life. Ideal beauty, like ideal genius, dwells apart, as though by compulsion; supremacy is solitude. But leaving this symbolic side of the matter, I cannot see why this statue should not be the text for yet another poem. Treated in the grave and chaste manner as a serious "thing of beauty," to be for ever applauded and enjoyed, it can give no offence but to the purblind and the prurient. For neither of these classes have I ever written or will I ever write. "Loathsome and abominable" and full of "unspeakable foulnesses" must be that man's mind who could here discern evil; unclean and inhuman the animal which could suck from this mystical rose of ancient loveliness the foul and rancid juices of an obscene fancy. It were a scavenger's office

---

But Shelley had not studied purity in the school of reviewers. It is well for us that we have teachers able to enlighten our darkness, or Heaven knows into what error such as he, or such as I, might not fall. We might even, in time, come to think it possible to enjoy the naked beauty of a statue or a picture without any virtuous vision behind it of a filthy fancy:[27] which would be immoral.

to descend with torch or spade into such depths of mental sewerage, to plunge or peer into subterranean sloughs of mind impossible alike to enlighten or to cleanse.

I have now gone over the poems which, as I hear, have incurred most blame; whether deservedly or not, I have shown. For the terms in which certain critics have clothed their sentiments I bear them no ill-will: they are welcome for me to write unmolested, as long as they keep to simple ribaldry. I hope it gives them amusement; I presume it brings them profit; I know it does not affect me. Absolute falsehood may, if it be worth while, draw down contradiction and disproof; but the mere calling of bad names is a child's trick, for which the small fry of the press should have a child's correction at the hands of able editors; standing as these gentlemen ought to do in a parental or pedagogic relation to their tender charges. They have, by all I see and hear, been sufficiently scurrilous—one or two in particular.

> However, from one crime they are exempt;
> They do not strike a brother, striking *me*.

I will only throw them one crumb of advice in return; I fear the alms will be of no avail, but it shall not be withheld:—

> Why grudge them lotus-leaf and laurel,
>   O toothless mouth or swinish maw,
> Who never grudged you bells and coral,
>   Who never grudged you troughs and straw?
>
> Lie still in kennel, sleek in stable,
>   Good creatures of the stall or sty;
> Shove snouts for crumbs below the table;
>   Lie still; and rise not up to lie.

To all this, however, there is a grave side. The question at issue is wider than any between a single writer and his critics, or it might well be allowed to drop. It is this: whether or not the first and last requisite of art is to give no offence; whether or not all that cannot be lisped in the nursery or fingered in the schoolroom is therefore to be cast out of the library; whether or not the domestic circle is to be for all men and writers the outer limit and extreme horizon of their world of work. For to this we have come; and all students of art must face the matter as it stands. Who has not heard it asked, in a final and triumphant tone, whether this book or that can be read aloud by her mother to a young girl? whether such and such a picture can properly be exposed to the eyes of young persons? If you reply that this is nothing to the point, you fall at once into the ranks of the immoral. Never till now, and nowhere but in England, could so monstrous an absurdity rear for one moment its deformed and eyeless head. In no past century were artists ever bidden to work on these terms; nor are they now, except among us. The disease, of course, afflicts the meanest members of the body with most virulence. Nowhere is cant at once so foul-mouthed and so tight-laced as in the penny, twopenny, threepenny, or sixpenny press. Nothing is so favourable to the undergrowth of real indecency as this overshadowing foliage of fictions, this artificial network of proprieties. *L'Arioste rit au soleil, l'Arétin ricane à l'ombre.* The whiter the sepulchre without, the ranker the rottenness within. Every touch of plaster is a sign of advancing decay. The virtue of our critical journals is a dowager of somewhat dubious antecedents: every day that thins and shrivels her cheek thickens and hardens the paint on it; she consumes more chalk and ceruse than would serve a whole courtful of crones. "It is to be presumed," certainly, that in her case "all is not sweet, all is not sound." The taint on her fly-blown reputation is hard to overcome by patches and perfumery. Literature, to be worthy of men, must be large, liberal, sincere; and cannot be chaste if it be prudish. Purity and prudery cannot keep house together. Where free speech and fair play are interdicted, foul hints and vile[28] suggestions are hatched into fetid life. And if literature indeed is not to deal with the full life of man and the whole nature of things, let it be cast aside with the rods and rattles of childhood. Whether it affect to teach or to amuse, it is equally trivial and contemptible to us; only less so than the charge of immorality. Against how few really great names has not this small and dirt-encrusted pebble been thrown! A reputation seems imperfect without this tribute[29] also: one jewel is wanting to the crown. It is good to be praised by those whom all men should praise[30]; it is better to be reviled by those whom all men should scorn.[31]

Various chances and causes must have combined to produce a

state of faith or feeling which would turn all art and literature "into the line of children." One among others may be this: where the heaven of invention holds many stars at once, there is no fear that the highest and largest will either efface or draw aside into its orbit all lesser lights. Each of these takes its own way and sheds its proper lustre. But where one alone is dominant in heaven, it is encircled by a pale procession of satellite moons, filled with shallow and stolen radiance. Thus, with English versifiers now, the idyllic form is alone in favour.[32] The one great and prosperous poet of the time has given out the tune, and the hoarser choir takes it up. His highest lyrical work remains unimitated, being in the main inimitable. But the trick of tone which suits an idyl is easier to assume; and the note has been struck so often that the shrillest songsters can affect to catch it up. We have idyls good and bad, ugly and pretty; idyls of the farm and the mill; idyls of the dining-room and the deanery; idyls of the gutter and the gibbet. If the Muse of the minute will not feast with "gigmen" and their wives, she must mourn with costermongers and their trulls. I fear the more ancient Muses are guests at neither house of mourning nor house of feasting.

For myself, I begrudge no man his taste or his success; I can enjoy and applaud all good work, and would always, when possible, have the workman paid in full. There is much excellent and some admirable verse among the poems of the day: to none has it given more pleasure than to me, and from none, had I been a man of letters to whom the ways were open, would it have won heartier applause. I have never been able to see what should attract men to the profession of criticism but the noble pleasure of praising. But I have no right to claim a place in the silver flock of idyllic swans. I have never worked for praise or pay, but simply by impulse, and to please myself; I must therefore, it is to be feared, remain where I am, shut out from the communion of these. At all events, I shall not be hounded into emulation of other men's work by the baying of unleashed beagles. There are those with whom I do not wish to share the praise of their praisers. I am content to abide a far different judgment:—

> I write as others wrote
> On Sunium's height.[33]

I need not be over-careful to justify my ways in other men's eyes; it is enough for me that they also work after their kind, and earn the suffrage, as they labour after the law, of their own people. The idyllic form is best for domestic and pastoral poetry. It is naturally on a lower level than that of tragic or lyric verse. Its gentle and maidenly lips are somewhat narrow for the stream and somewhat cold[34] for the fire of song. It is very fit for the sole diet of girls; not very fit for the sole sustenance of men.

When England has again such a school of poetry, so headed and so followed, as she has had at least twice before, or as France has now; when all higher forms of the various art are included within the larger limits of a stronger race; then, if such a day should ever rise or return upon us, it will be once more remembered that the office of adult art is neither puerile nor feminine, but virile; that its purity is not that of the cloister or the harem; that all things are good in its sight, out of which good work may be produced. Then the press will be as impotent as the pulpit to dictate the laws and remove the landmarks of art; and those will be laughed at who demand from one thing the qualities of another—who seek for sermons in sonnets and morality in music. Then all accepted work will be noble and chaste in the wider masculine sense, not truncated and curtailed, but outspoken and full-grown; art will be pure by instinct and fruitful by nature, no clipped and forced growth of unhealthy heat and unnatural air; all baseness and all triviality will fall off from it, and be forgotten; and no one will then need to assert, in defence of work done for the work's sake, the simple laws of his art which no one will then be permitted to impugn.

A. C. SWINBURNE.

UNDER THE MICROSCOPE

WE live in an age when not to be scientific is to be nothing; the man untrained in science, though he should speak with the tongues of men and of angels, though he should know all that man may know of the history of men and their works in time past, though he should have nourished on the study of their noblest examples in art and literature whatever he may have of natural intelligence, is but a pitiable and worthless pretender in the sight of professors to whom natural science is not a mean but an end; not an instrument of priceless worth for the mental workman, but a result in itself satisfying and final, a substitute in place of an auxiliary, a sovereign in lieu of an ally, a goal instead of a chariot. It is not enough in their eyes to admit that all study[1] of details is precious or necessary to help us to a larger and surer knowledge of the whole; that without the invaluable support and illumination of practical research and physical science, the human intellect must still as of old go limping and blinking on its way nowhither, lame of one foot at best and blind of one eye; the knowledge of bones and stones is good not merely as a part of that general knowledge of nature inward as well as outward, human as well as other, towards which the mind would fain make its way yet a little and again a little further through all obstruction of error and suffusion of mystery; it is in the bones and stones themselves, not in man at all or the works of man, that we are to find the ultimate satisfaction and the crowning interest of our studies. Not because the study of such things will rid us of traditional obstacles that lay in the way of free and fruitful thought, will clear the air of mythologic malaria, will purge the spiritual city from religious pestilence; not because each one new certitude attained must involve the overthrow of more illusions than one, and every fact we can gather brings us by so much nearer to the truth we seek, serves as it were for a single brick or beam in the great house of knowledge that all students and thinkers who have served the world or are

35

to serve it have borne or will bear their part in helping to construct. The facts are not of value simply because they serve the truth; nor are there so many mansions as once we may have thought in this house of truth, nor so many ministers in its service. It is vain to reply, while admitting that truth cannot be reached by men who take no due account of facts, that each fact is not all the truth, each limb is not all the body, each thought is not all the mind; and that even men (if such there be) ignorant of everything but what other men have written may possibly not be ignorant of everything worth knowledge, destitute of every capacity worth exercise. One study alone, and one form of study, is worthy the time and the respect of men who would escape the contempt of their kind. Impressed by this consideration—impelled by late regret and tardy ambition to atone if possible for lost time and thought misspent—I have determined to devote at least a spare hour to the science of comparative entomology; and propose here to set down in a few loose notes the modest outcome of my morning's researches.

Every beginner must be content to start from the lowest point —to begin at the bottom if he ever hopes to reach the top, or indeed to gain any trustworthy foothold at all. Our studies should therefore in this case also be founded on a preliminary examination of things belonging to the class of the infinitely little; and of these we shall do well to take up first such samples for inspection as may happen to lie nearest at hand. As the traveller who may desire to put to profit in the interest of this science his enforced night's lodging "in the worst inn's worst room" must take for his subjects of study the special or generic properties of such parasites as may leap or creep about his place of rest or unrest; so the lodger in the house of art or literature who for once may wish in like manner to utilize his waste moments must not scorn to pay some passing attention to the varieties of the critical tribe. But if the traveller be a man of truly scientific mind, he will be careful to let no sense of irritation impair the value and accuracy of his research. Such evidence of sensitiveness or suffering would not indeed imply that he thought otherwise or more highly of these than of other parasites;[2] it is but a nameless thing after all, unmentionable as well as anonymous, that has pierced his skin if it be really pierced, or inflamed his blood if it be indeed inflamed; but those are the best travellers whose natures are not made of such penetrable or inflammable stuff. A critic is, at worst, but what Blake once painted—the ghost of a flea; and the man must be very tough of skin or very tender of spirit who would not rather have to do with the shadow than the substance. The phantom confessed to the painter that he would destroy the world if his power were commensurate with his will; but then it was not. Exactly as much power as was given to Blake's sitter (if that term be in his case allowable) to destroy the world is given to the critic to destroy the creator; exactly so much of that enviable power has a Pontmartin (for example) on Hugo and Balzac, or an Austin (for example) on Tennyson and Browning, or a Buchanan (for example) on any living thing. Considering which fact, all men of sense and self-respect will assuredly be of one mind with the greatest Englishman left among us to represent the mighty breed of our elders since Landor went to find his equals and rejoin his kin among the Grecian shades "where Orpheus and where Homer are." It is long since Mr. Carlyle expressed his opinion that if any poet or other literary creature could really be "killed off by one critique" or many, the sooner he was so despatched the better; a sentiment in which I for one humbly but heartily concur.

There is one large and interesting class of the critical race which unfortunately has hitherto in great measure defied the researches of science. Any collector who by any fair means[3] has secured a sample of this species may naturally be prone to exhibit it with pride among the choicer spoils of his museum; not indeed for its beauty, and certainly not for its rarity; it may be seen in every hedge and every morass, but the difficulty is to determine and distinguish any single specimen by its proper and recognizable name. This species is composed of the critics known only as anonyms. Being anonymous, how can its members be classified by any scientific system of nomenclature? A mere dabbler in the science like myself must not hope[4] at his first start to secure a prize of this kind; such trophies are not for the hand of a beginner. The sciolist who thinks to affix its label and assign its place to any one specimen of the tribe will be liable to grave error. In the grand pantomime of anonymous criticism the actors shift their parts and change their faces so suddenly that no one whose life has not been spent behind the scenes can hope to verify his guess at the wearer of such or such a mask. We see Harlequin Virtue make love to the goddess Grundy, and watch if we can without yawning the raddled old columbine Cant perform her usual pirouettes in the ballet of morality; we have hardly heart to sit out, though revived on so rotten a stage by express desire, the screaming farce of religion; and after all we are never sure whether it was Clown or Pantaloon whom we heard snuffling and wheezing in the side-scenes. We go for instance to the old Quarterly Theatre, confident that we shall see and hear the old actors in their old parts, or at least some worthy successor and heir to the sound stage traditions of the house; and indeed we find much the same show of decoration and much the same style of declamation as ever; but we had a tender and pardonable weakness for the old faces and the old voices; and now we cannot even tell if they are here or no; whether the part taken in the first act by an old familiar friend is not continued in the second by a new performer of much promise and ability, remarkable for his more than apish or parrot-like dexterity in picking up and reproducing the tricks and phrases, tones and gestures, of the stage-struck veteran in whose place he stands; but not the man we came to see. We cannot hang upon the actor's lips with the same breathless attention when we know not whether it be[5] master or pupil who speaks behind the mask. What in the elder actor was a natural gift of personation is but an empirical knack of imitation in his copyist. At least we would fain know for certain whether the moral gambols performed before us are those of the old showman or his ape. Or say that we come thither as to church or lecture: it cannot tend to edification that we should not know whom we sit under. We are distracted throughout sermon-time by doubts whether the veiled preacher be indeed as we thought a man of gravity from his youth upwards, a holy and austere minister of the altar, a Nazarite of lifelong sanctity, a venerable athlete of the Church, about whose past there can be no more question than about his right to speak as one ordained to apostolic office and succession by laying on of hands; or haply a neophyte from the outer court,

a deacon but newly made reverend, an interloper even it may be or
a schismatic: the doubt is nothing short of agony. Imagine,[6]
gathered about the pulpit, a little flock of penitents who come
gladly to be admonished, who ask nothing better than to be
convinced of sin, who listen humbly to the pastoral rebuke, accept
meekly the paternal chastisement, of the preacher who summons
them before him to judgment; what will be their consternation if
they have cause to suspect that it is not an orthodox shepherd of
souls whose voice of warning is in their ears, but an intruder[7] who
has climbed into the sheepfold! Clown masquerading in the guise
of Pantaloon; and in place of the man of God at whose admoni-
tion the sinner was wont to tremble with Felix, perhaps a comic
singer, a rhymester of boyish burlesque; there is no saying who
may not usurp the pulpit when once the priestly office and the
priestly vesture have passed into other than consecrated hands.
For instance, we hear in October, say, a discourse on Byron and
Tennyson; we are struck by the fervour and unction of the
preacher; we feel, like Satan, how awful goodness is, and see
virtue in her shape how lovely; see, and pine our loss, if haply we
too have fallen; we stand abashed at the reflection that never till
this man came to show us did we perceive the impurity of a poet
who can make his heroine "so familiar with male objects of desire"
as to allude to such a person as an odalisque "in good society";
we are ashamed to remember that never till now did we duly
appreciate the chastity of Dudù and her comrades, as contrasted
with the depravity of the Princess Ida and her collegians;[8] we
blush, if a blush be left in us, to hear on such authority "that
exception might be taken without excess of prudery to 'The Sisters,'" and to think that we should ever have got by heart, without a thought of evil to alloy the delight of admiration, a poem "in
which sensual passion is coarsely blended with the sense of injured honour and revenge." We read, and regret that ever the
fascination of verse should have so effectually closed our eyes and
ears against all perception of these deplorable qualities in a poet
whose name we have cherished from our childhood; and as we
read there rises before us the august and austere vision of a man
well stricken in years, but of life unspotted from the world, pure
as a child in word and thought, stern as an apostle in his rebuke

of youthful wantonness or maturer levity; we feel that in his presence no one would venture on a loose jest or equivocal allusion, no one dream of indulgence in foolish talking and jesting, which (as he would assuredly remind the offender), we know on the highest authority, is not convenient; and we call reverently to mind the words of a poet, in which the beauty of a virtuous old age is affectingly set forth.

> How sweet is chastity in hoary hairs!
>   How venerable the speech of an old man
> Pure as a maiden's, and a cheek that wears
>   In age the blush it wore when youth began!
> The lip still saintly with a sense of prayers
>   Angelical, with power to bless or ban,
> Stern to rebuke tongues heedless of control,—
> A virgin elder with a vestal soul.

Or perchance there may rise to our own lips the equally impressive tribute of a French writer at the same venerable shrine.

> Vieillard, ton âme austère est une âme d'élite:
> Et quand la conscience humaine a fait faillite,
> Ta voix sévère est comme un rappel qu'on entend
> Sonner du fond de l'ombre où le sort nous attend.
> L'appétit nu, la chair affamée et rieuse,
> Source âpre et basse où boit la jeunesse oublieuse,
> La luxure cynique au regard fauve et vil,
> Rentre, à ton aspect, comme un chien dans son chenil.
> Jamais le rire impur ne vint souiller de fange
> Ta lèvre où luit le feu de l'apôtre et de l'ange.
> Le satyre au chant rauque a peur devant tes yeux;
> Le vice à ton abord frémit silencieux;
> Et la neige qui pleut sur ta tête qui penche,
> Quand on a vu ton cœur, ne semble plus si blanche.

I know not whether the rebuke of venerable virtue had power to affect the callous conscience of the "hoarse-voiced satyr" thus convicted of "the depth of ill-breeding and bad taste"; but I cannot doubt that when in January a like parable was taken up in the same quarter against certain younger offenders, the thought that the same voice with the same weight of judgment in its tones was

Vuillard, ton âme austère est une âme d'élite:

Et quand la conscience humaine a fait faillite,

Ta voix sévère est comme un rappel qu'on entend

Sourdre du fond de l'ombre où le sort nous attend.

L'appétit [nu] ..., la chair affamée et ...,

Source âpre où ... et boit la jeunesse oublieuse,

La luxure cynique au regard jaune et vil,

Rentre à ton aspect comme un chien dans son chenil.

Jamais le rire ... ne vient souiller de fange

Ta lèvre haletée à des ... d'archange.

Le satyre au chant ... à feu ... ses yeux

Le vice à ton regard ... silencieux;

Et la neige qui pleut sur ta tête qui penche,

Quand on a ... ton cœur en semble plus si blanche.

From the Manuscript of *Under the Microscope*

raised to denounce them must have struck cold to their hearts while it brought the blood to their cheeks. The likeness in turn of phrase and inflexion of voice was perfect; the air of age and authority, if indeed it was but assumed, was assumed with faultless and exquisite fidelity; the choice of points for attack and words to attack with was as nearly as might be identical. "No terms of condemnation could be too strong," so rang that "terrible voice of most just judgment," "for the revolting picturesqueness of A's description of the sexual relation"; it was illustrated by sacramental symbols of "gross profanity"; it gave evidence of "emasculate obscenity,"* and a deliberate addiction to "the worship of Priapus." The virtuous journalist, I have observed, is remarkably fond of Priapus; his frequent and forcible allusions to "the honest garden-god" recur with a devout iteration to be found in no other worshipper; for one such reference in graver or lighter verse you may find a score in prose of the moral and critical sort. Long since, in that incomparable satiric essay which won for its young author the deathless applause of Balzac—"magnifique préface d'un livre magnifique"—Théophile Gautier had occasion to remark on the intimate familiarity of the virtuous journalist with all the occult obscenities of literature, the depth and width of range which his studies in that line would seem to have taken, if we might judge by his numerous and ready citations of the titles of indecent books with which he would associate the title of the book reviewed. This problematic intimacy the French poet finds no plausible way to explain; and with it we must leave the other problem on which I have touched above, in the hope that some day a more advanced stage of scientific inquiry will produce men competent to resolve it. Meantime we may remark again the very twang of the former preacher in the voice which now denounces to our ridicule B's "want of sense," while it invokes our disgust as fire from heaven on his "want of decency," in the use of a type borrowed from the Christian mythology and

---

* "*Climène.* Il a une obscénité qui n'est pas supportable.

Elise. Comment dites-vous ce mot-là, madame?

Climène. Obscénité, madame.

Elise. Ah! mon Dieu! obscénité. Je ne sais ce que ce mot veut dire; mais je le trouve le plus joli du monde."

MOLIERE, *La Critique de l'Ecole des Femmes*, sc. 3.

applied to actual doings and sufferings; and once more we surely seem to "know the sweet Roman hand" that sets down our errors in its register, when the critic remarks on the absurd inconsequence of a poet who addresses by name and denounces in person a god in whose personal existence he does not believe. In the name of all divine persons that ever did or did not exist, what on earth or in heaven would the critic in such a case expect? Is it from the believers in a particular god or gods that he would look for exposure and denunciation of their especial creed? Would it be[9] natural and rational for a man to attack and denounce a name he believes in or a person he adores, unnatural and irrational to attack and denounce by name a godhead or a gospel he finds incredible and abominable to him? When a great poetess apostrophized the gods of Hellas as dead, was the form of apostrophe made inconsequent and absurd by the fact that she did not believe them to be alive? For a choicer specimen of preacher's logic than this we might seek long without finding it. But we must not be led away into argument or answer addressed to the subjects of our research, while as yet the work before us remains unaccomplished. The self-imposed task is simple and severe; we would merely submit to the analysis of scientific examination the examiners of other men, bring[10] under our microscope, as it were, the telescopic apparatus which they on their side bring to investigate from below things otherwise invisible to them, as they would be imperceptible from above but for the microscopic lens which science enables us in turn to apply to themselves and their appliances. As to answer, if any workman who has done any work of his own should be asked why he does not come forward to take up any challenge flung down to him, or sweep out of his way any litter of lies and insults that may chance to encumber it for a moment, his reply for his fellows and himself to those who suggest that they should engage in such a warfare might perhaps run somewhat thus: Are we cranes or mice, that we should give battle to the frogs or the pigmies? Examine them we may at our leisure, in the pursuit of natural history, if our studies should chance to have taken that turn; but as we cannot, when they speak out of the darkness, tell frog from frog by his croak, or pigmy from pigmy by his features, and are thus liable at every moment

to the most unscientific errors in definition, it seems best to seek
no further for quaint or notable examples of a kind which we
cannot profitably attempt to classify. Not without regret, therefore, we resign to more adventurous explorers the whole range of
the anonymous wilderness, and confine our own modest researches
to the limits within which we may trust ourselves to make no
grave mistakes of kind. But within these limits, too, there is a race
which defies even scientific handling, and for a reason yet graver
and more final. Among writers who publish and sign such things
as they have to say about or against their contemporaries, there
is still, as of old, a class which is protected against response or
remark, as (to use an apt example of Macaulay's) "the skunk is
protected against the hunters. It is safe, because it is too filthy to
handle, and too noisome even to approach." To this class belong
the creatures known to naturalists by the generic term of coprophagi; a generation which derives its sustenance from the unclean
matter which produced it, and lives on the very stuff of which it
was born:

> They are no vipers, yet they feed
> On mother-dung which did them breed:

and under this head we find ranked, for example, the workers and
dealers in false and foul ware for minor magazines and newspapers, to whom now that they know their ears to be safe from
the pillory and their shoulders from the scourge there is no restraint and no reply applicable but the restraint and the reply of
the law which imposes on their kind the brand of a shameful
penalty; and it is not every day that an honest man will care to
come forward and procure its infliction on some representative
rascal of the tribe at the price of having to swear that the spittle
aimed at his face came from the lips of a liar; that he has not lived
on such terms of intimacy with the honest gentleman at the bar
that the confidential and circumstantial report given of his life
and opinions, habits and theories, person and conversation, is
absolutely to be taken for gospel by the curious in such matters.
The age of Pope is past, and we no longer expect a man of note
to dive into the common sink of letters for the purpose of un-
earthing from its native place and nailing up by the throat in sight
of day any chance vermin that may slink out in foul weather to

assail him. The celebrity of Oldmixon and Curll is no longer attainable by dint of scurrilous persistency in provocation; in vain may the sons of the sewer look up with longing eyes after the hope of such peculiar immortality as that bestowed by Swift on the names of Whiston and Ditton: upon their upturned faces there will fall no drop or flake of such unfragrant fame. When some one told Dr. Johnson that a noted libeller had been publicly kicked in the streets of Dublin, his answer was to the effect that he was glad to hear of so clever a man rising so rapidly in the world; when he was in London, no one at whom his personalities might be launched ever thought it worth while to kick him. There are writers apparently consumed by a vain ambition to emulate the rise in life thus achieved by one of their precursors; and it takes them some time to discover, and despond as they admit, that such luck is not always to be looked for. Some, as in fond hope of such notice, assume the gay patrician in their style, while others in preference[11] affect the honest plebeian; but in neither case do they succeed in attracting the touch which might confer celebrity; the very means they take to draw it down on themselves suffice to keep it off; at each fresh emanation or exhalation of their malodorous souls it becomes more clearly impossible for man to approach them even "with stopped nostril and glove-guarded hand." When the dirtier lackeys of literature come forward in cast clothes to revile or to represent their betters, to caricature by personation or by defamation the masters of the house, men do not now look at them and pass by; they pass without looking, and have neither eye for the pretentions nor cudgel for the backs of the Marquis de Mascarille and the Vicomte de Jodelet.

Of such creatures, then, even though they be nothing if not critical, we do not propose to treat; but only of such examples of the critical kind as may be shown in public without apology by the collector, not retained (if retained at all) for necessary purposes of science on the most private shelves of his cabinet. Among these more presentable classes there is considerable diversity of kind to be traced by the discerning eye, though many signs and symptoms be in almost all cases identical. There is the critic who believes that no good thing can come out of such a Nazarene generation as the men of his own time; and there is the critic who believes first in himself alone, and through himself in the gods or godlings of his worship and the eggs or nestlings hatched or addled under the incubation of his patronage. Between these two kinds there rages a natural warfare as worthy of a burlesque poet as any batrachomyomachy that ever was fought out. It is no bad sport to watch through a magnifying glass the reciprocal attack and defence of their little lines of battle and posts of vantage—

> Et, dans la goutte d'eau, les guerres du volvoce
> Avec le vibrion.

In all times there have been men in plenty convinced of the decadence of their own age; of which they have not usually been classed among the more distinguished children. We are happy in having among us a critic of some culture and of much noisy pertinacity who will serve well enough to represent the tribe. I distinguish his book on "The Poetry of the Period," supplemented as I take it to be by further essays in criticism thrown out in the same line, not for any controversial purpose, and assuredly with no view of attempting to answer or to confute the verdicts therein issued, to prove by force of reasoning or proclaim by force of rhetoric that the gulf between past and present is less deep and distinct than this author believes and alleges it to be; that the dead were not so far above the average type of men, that the living are not so far below it, as writers of this type have always been equally prone to maintain. I have little taste for such controversy and little belief in its value; but even if the diversion of arguing as to what sort of work should be done or is being done or has been were in my mind preferable to the business of doing as seems to me best whatever work my hand finds to do, I should not enter into a debate in which my own name was mixed up. Whether the men of this time be men of a great age or a small is not a matter to be decided by their own assertion or denial; but in any case a man of any generation can keep his hand and foot out of the perpetual wrangle and jangle of "the petty fools of rhyme who shriek and sweat in pigmy jars," which recur in every age of literature with a pitiful repetition of the same cries and catchwords. I could never understand, and certainly I could never

admire, the habit of mind or the form of energy which finds work
and vent in demonstration or proclamation of the incompetence
for all good of other men; but much less can I admire or understand the impulse which would thrust a man forward to shriek
out in reply some assertion of his own injured merit and the value
of the work which he for instance has done for the world even
in this much maligned generation. No man can prove or disprove
his own worth except by his own work; and is it after all so
grave a question to determine whether the merit of that be more
or less? The world in its time will not want for great men, though
he in his time be never so small; and if, small or great, he be a
man of any courage or of any sense, he will find comfort and
delight enough to last his time in the quite unmistakeably and
indubitably great work of other men past or present, without any
such irritable prurience of appetite for personal fame or hankering retrospection of regret for any foiled ambitions of his own.
This temper of mind, which all men should be able to attain, must
preserve him from the unprofitable and ignoble sufferings of
fools and cowards; and self-contempt, the appointed scourge of
all envious egotists, will have no sting for him. And once aware
that his actual merit or demerit is no such mighty matter in the
world's eye, and the success or failure of his own life's work in
any line of thought or action is probably not of any incalculable
importance to his own age or the next, the man who has learnt
not to care overmuch about his real rank and relation to other
workmen as greater or less than they, will hardly trouble himself
overmuch about the opinions held or expressed as to that rank
and relation. What is said of him must be either true or false;
if false, he would simply be a fool—if true, he would also be a
coward—to wish it unsaid; for a lie in the end hurts none but the
liar, and a truth is at all times profitable to all. In any case then
it can do him no damage; for good work and worthy to last is
indestructible; and to destroy with all due speed any destructible
person or book not worthy to last is no injury to any one whatever, but the greatest service that can be done to the book and
the writer themselves, not less—nay perhaps much more—than to
the rest of the poor world which has no mind to be "pestered with
such water-flies—diminutives of nature." In a word, whatever is

fit to live is safe to live, and whatever is not fit to live is sure to die, though all men should swear and struggle to the contrary; and it is hard to say which of these is the more consoling certainty. I shall not, therefore, select any book for refutation of its principle, but merely for examination of its argument; my only aim being to test by this simplest of means what may be its purport and its weight. I find for instance that Mr. Austin, satirist and critic by profession, writing with a plain emphatic energy and decision which make his essays on the poetry of the period easily and pleasantly readable by students of the minute, maintains throughout his book the opposition between two leading figures; the same figures since chosen for the same purpose by the venerable monitor at whose feet we have already sat attentive and shrunk rebuked. In Byron the mighty past and in Tennyson the petty present is incarnate; other giants of less prominence are ranked behind the former, other pigmies of less proportion are gathered about the latter; but throughout it is assumed that no fairer example than either could be found of the best that his age had to show. We may admit for a moment the assumption that Byron was as indisputably at the head of his own generation, as indisputably its fittest and fullest representative, as we all allow Mr. Tennyson to be of his; and this assumption we may admit, because Mr. Austin is so good and complete a type of one class of the great critical kind, that by such a concession we may enable ourselves to get a clear view and a firm grasp of some definable principles of criticism; and thus to examine as we proposed the arguments on which these are based, and which we approach with no prepense design or premeditated aim to corroborate or to confute them, but simply to investigate. With a writer less clear and less forcible in purpose and in style we might not hope to get sight or hold of any principle at all; but this one, right or wrong and wise or unwise, at least does not babble to no purpose whatever like the "blind mouths" that prattle by mere chance of impulse or of habit. First then we observe that he offers us samples of either poet's work with a great show of fairness in the choice of representative passages; he bids us, like a new Hamlet rebuking the weakness and the shame of his mother-age, look here upon this picture and on this; and a counterfeit presentment it is indeed

that he shows us. Taking an instance from his final essay, the sum-
mary and result of the book, we find a few lines from a slight
poem of Mr. Tennyson's extreme youth, and one which is by no
means a fair example of even his earliest manner, set against the
most famous and the finest passage but one in "Childe Harold"
—the description of an Alpine thunderstorm. With equal justice
and with equal profit we might pick out the worst refuse of dolor-
ous doggrel from the rubbish-heaps of "Hours of Idleness" or
"Hebrew Melodies"—say that version of the 137th Psalm so
admirably parodied by Landor, of which the indignant shade of
Hopkins might howl rejection, while the milder ghost of Brady
would dissolve in air if accused of it—that or such another rag
or shard of verse from the sweepings of Byron's bad work—and
set it against the majestic close of the "Lotus-eaters" or some
passage of most finished exaltation from "In Memoriam." But
the critic has yet a better trick than this, ingenious and ingenuous
as it is, to pervert the judgment of those who might chance to take
his evidence on trust. He has copied accurately the short passage
chosen to show the immature genius of Tennyson at its feeblest;
but the longer passage chosen, and very well chosen, to show the
mature genius of Byron at its mightiest, he has been careful to
alter and improve by the studious and judicious excision of two
whole intervening stanzas; the second good in itself, but introduced by one stolen from Coleridge and deformed almost past
recognition from a thing of supreme and perfect beauty into a
formless and tuneless mass of clumsy verbosity and floundering
incoherence. Even thus garbled and disembowelled, the passage,
noble and delightful as in the main it is, stands yet defaced by two
lines which no poet of the first order could have committed; two
lines showing such hideous deficiency of instinct, such helpless
want of the imaginative sense which in the highest poets is as
strong and as sure to preserve from error as to impel towards
perfection, that any man with an inner ear for that twin-born
music of coequal thought and word without which there is no
high poetry possible, must feel with all regret that here is not
one of the poets who can be trusted by those who would enjoy
them; but one who at the highest and smoothest of his full-
winged flight is liable to some horrible collapse or flap of a dis-

located pinion. The first offence is that monstrous simile—monstrous at once and mean—of "the light of a dark eye in woman," which must surely have been stolen from Hayley; if even the author of the "Triumphs of Temper" can ever have thought a woman's eye an apt and noble likeness for the whole heaven of night in storm. This is the true sign of flawed or defective imagination; that a man should think, because the comparison of a woman's eye to a stormy night may be striking and ennobling, therefore the inverted comparison of a stormy night to a woman's eye must also be proper and impressive. The second offence is yet worse; it is that incomparable phrase of the mountains "rejoicing o'er a young earthquake's birth," which again I should conjecture to have been borrowed from Elkanah Settle; it is really much in the manner of some lines cited from that poet by Scott in his notes on Dryden. A young earthquake! why not a young toothache, a young spasm, or a young sneeze? We see the difference between sense and nonsense, pure imagination and mere turbid energy, when we turn to a phrase of Shelley's on the same subject:[12]

> Is this the scene
> Where the old earthquake-demon taught her young
> Ruin?

There is a symbol conceivable by the mind's eye, noble and coherent. But to such critics as Mr. Austin it is all one; for them there are no such fine-drawn distinctions between words with a meaning and words without—with them, as with poor Elkanah, "if they rhyme and rattle, all is well." This selection and collocation of fragmentary passages, it will be said, is not the best way to attain a fair and serious estimate of either poet's worth or station; Byron may be or may not be as much greater than Tennyson as the critic shall please, but this is not a sufficient process of proof. Nor assuredly do I think it is; but the method chosen is none of mine; it is the method chosen by the critic whom for the moment I follow to examine his system of criticism. His choice of an instance is designedly injurious to the poet whom it shows at his weakest; but it seems to me, however undesignedly, not much less injurious to the poet whom it shows at his strongest. Such is frequently the effect of such tactics, the net result and upshot of such an advocate's good intentions. It will hardly be supposed that I have dwelt with any delight on the disparaging scrutiny of an otherwise admirable extract from a poet in whose praise I should have said enough elsewhere to stand clear of any possible charge of injustice or incompetence to enjoy his glorious and ardent genius; I have dwelt indeed with a genuine delight on a task far different from this—the task of praising with all my might, and if with superfluous yet certainly with sincere expression, his magnificent quality of communion with the great things of nature and translation of the joyous and terrible sense they give us of her living infinity, which has been given in like degree to no living poet but one greater far than Byron—the author of the *Contemplations* and the *Légende des Siècles*. This tribute, however inadequate and however unnecessary, was paid to the memory of Byron before ever his latest English panegyrist laid lance in rest against all comers in defence of his fame; using meantime that fame as a stalking-horse behind which to shoot at the fame of others. And as to his assumed office of spokesman on behalf of Byron—a very noble office it would be if there were any need or place for it—we cannot but ask who gave him his credentials as advocate or apologist for a poet whose fame was to all seeming as secure as any man's? Is the name of Byron fallen so low that such a style of advocacy and such a class of counsel must be sought out to revive its drooping credit and refresh its withered honours? *Quis vituperavit?* Has any one attacked his noble memory as a poet or a man, except here and there a journalist of the tribe of Levi or Tartuffe, or a blatant Bassarid of Boston, a rampant Mænad of Massachusetts? To wipe off the froth of falsehood from the foaming lips of inebriated virtue, when fresh from the sexless orgies of morality and reeling from the delirious riot of religion, may doubtless be a charitable office; but it is no proof of critical sense or judgment to set about the vindication of a great man as though his repute could by any chance be widely or durably affected by the confidences exchanged in the most secret place and hour of their sacred rites, far from the clamour of public halls and platforms made hoarse with holiness,

Ubi sacra sancta acutis ululatibus agitant,

between two whispering priestesses of whatever god presides over the most vicious parts of virtue, the most shameless rites of modesty, the most rancorous forms of forgiveness—the very Floralia of evangelical faith and love. That two such spirits, naked and not ashamed, should so have met and mingled in the communion of calumny, have taken each with devout avidity her part in the obscene sacrament of hate, her share in the graceless eucharist of evil-speaking, is not more wonderful or more important than that the elder devotee should have duped the younger into a belief that she alone had been admitted to partake of a fouler feast than that eaten in mockery at a witch's sabbath, a wafer more impure from a table more unspeakably polluted—the bread of slander from the altar of madness or malignity, the bitter poison of a shrine on which the cloven tongue of hell-fire might ever be expected to reappear with the return of some infernal Pentecost. All this is as natural and as insignificant as that the younger priestess on her part should since have trafficked in the unhallowed elements of their common and unclean mystery, have revealed for hire the unsacred secrets of no Eleusinian initiation. To whom can it matter that such a plume-plucked Celæno as this should come with all the filth and flutter of her kind to defile a grave which is safe and high enough above the abomination of her approach? Not, I should have thought, to those who hold most in honour all that was worthiest of men's honour in Byron. Surely he needs no defence against this posthumous conjugal effusion at second hand[13] of such a venomous and virulent charity as might shame the veriest Christian to have shown. And who else speaks evil of him but now and then some priest or pedagogue, frocked or unfrocked, in lecture or review? It should be remembered that a warfare carried into such quarters can bring honour or profit to no man. We are not accustomed to give back railing for railing that is flung at us from the pulpit or the street-corner. In the church as in the highway, the skirt significant of sex, be it sur-pliced or draggle-tailed, should suffice to protect the wearer from any reciprocity of vituperation. If it should ever be a clerical writer, whether of the regular or the secular order—an amateur who officiates by choice or by chance, or a registered official whose services are duly salaried—that may happen to review a book in which you may happen to have touched unawares on some naked nerve of his religious feeling or professional faith, you are not moved to any surprise or anger that he should liken you to a boy rolling in a puddle, or laugh at you in pity as he throws aside in disgust the proof of your fatuous ignorance; you know that this is the rhetoric or the reasoning of his kind, and that he means by it no more than a street-walker means by her curse as you pass by without response to her addresses; you remember that both alike may claim the freedom of the trade, and would as soon turn back to notice the one salutation as the other. Priests and prostitutes are a privileged class. Half of that axiom was long since laid down by Shelley; and it is not from any such quarter that he probably would have thought the fame of his friend in any such danger as to require much demonstration of championship. The worst enemies of Byron, as of all his kind, are not to be sought among such as these. They are his enemies who extol him for gifts which he had not and work which he could not do; who by dint of praising him for such qualities as were wanting to his genius call the attention of all men to his want of them; who are not content to pay all homage to his unsurpassed energy, his fiery eloquence, his fitful but gigantic force of spirit, his troubled but triumphant strength of soul; to his passionate courage, his noble wrath and pity and scorn, his bright and burning wit, the invincible vitality and sleepless vigour of action and motion which informs and imbues for us all his better part of work as with a sense of living and personal power; who are dissatisfied for him with this his just and natural part of praise, and by way of doing him right must needs rise up to glorify him for imagination, of which he had little, and harmony, of which he had none. Even when supporting himself as in "Manfred" on the wings of other poets, he cannot fly as straight or sing as true as they. It is not the mere fluid melody of dulcet and facile verse that is wanting to him; that he might want and be none the worse for want of it; it is the inner sense of harmony which cannot but speak in music, the innate and spiritual instinct of sweetness and fitness and exaltation which cannot but express itself in height and perfection of song. This divine concord is never infringed or violated in the stormiest symphonies of passion or imagination by any one of the supreme and sovereign poets: by Æschylus or Shakespeare, in the

tempest and agony of Prometheus or of Lear, it is no less surely
and naturally preserved than by Sophocles or by Milton in the
serener departure of Œdipus or the more temperate lament of
Samson. In a free country Mr. Austin or any other citizen may of
course take leave to set Byron beside Shelley or above him, as
Byron himself had leave to set Pope beside or above Shakespeare
and Milton; there is no harm done in either case even to Pope
or Byron, and assuredly there is no harm done to the greater
poets. The one thing memorable in the matter is the confidence
with which men who have absolutely no sense whatever of verbal
music will pronounce judgment on the subtlest questions relating
to that form of art. A man whose ear is conscious of no difference
between Offenbach and Beethoven does not usually stand up as
a judge of instrumental music; but there is no ear so hirsute or so
hard, so pointed or so long, that its wearer will not feel himself
qualified to pass sentence on the musical rank of any poet's verse,
the relative range and value of his metrical power or skill. If one
man says for instance that Shelley outsang all rivals while Byron
could not properly sing at all, and another man in reply is good
enough to inform him that what he meant to say and should have
said was that Byron could not shriek in falsetto like Shelley and
himself, the one betweenwhiles and the other at all times, what
answer or appeal is possible? The decision must be left to each
man's own sense of hearing, or to his estimate of the respective
worth of the two opinions given. I have always thought it somewhat hasty on the part of Sir Hugh Evans to condemn as "affectations" that phrase of Pistol's—"He hears with ears"; to hear with
ears is a gift by no means given to every man that wears them.
Our own meanwhile are still plagued with the cackle of such
judges on all points of art as those to whom Molière addressed
himself in vain—"qui blâment et louent tout à contre-sens, pren-
nent par où ils peuvent les termes de l'art qu'ils attrapent, et ne
manquent jamais de les estropier et de les mettre hors de place.
Hé! morbleu! messieurs,[14] taisez-vous. *Quand Dieu ne vous a pas
donné la connaissance d'une chose, n'apprêtez point à rire à ceux
qui vous entendent parler;* et songez qu'en ne disant mot on
croira peut-être que vous êtes d'habiles gens." Such another critic
as Mr. Austin is Herr Elze, the German biographer[15] who has been

sent among us after many days to inform our native ignorance that Byron was the greatest lyric poet of England. A few more such examples should have been vouchsafed us of "things not generally known"; such as these for instance: that our greatest dramatic poet was Dr. Johnson, our greatest comic poet was Sir Isaac Newton, our best amatory poet was Lord Bacon, our best religious poet was Lord Rochester, our best narrative poet was Joseph Addison, and our greatest epic poet was Tom Moore. Add to these the facts that Shakespeare's fame rests on his invention of gunpowder[16] and Milton's on his discovery of vaccination, and the student thus prepared and primed with useful knowledge will in time be qualified to match our instructor himself for accurate science of English literature, biographical or critical. It is a truth neither more nor less disputable than these that Byron was a great lyric poet; if the statements proposed above be true, then that also is true; if they be not, it also is not. He could no more have written a thoroughly good and perfect lyric, great or small, after the fashion of Hugo or after the fashion of Tennyson, than he could have written a page of Hamlet or of Paradise Lost. Even in the "Isles of Greece," excellent as the poem is throughout for eloquence and force, he stumbles into epigram or subsides into reflection with untimely lapse of rhetoric and unseemly change of note. The stanza on Miltiades is an almost vulgar instance of oratorical trick—"a very palpable hit" it might be on a platform, but it is a very palpable flaw in a lyric. Will it again be objected that such dissection as this of a poem is but a paltry and injurious form of criticism? Doubtless it is; but the test of true and great poetry is just this,[17] that it will endure, if need be, such a process of analysis or anatomy; that thus tried as in the fire and decomposed as in a crucible it comes out after all renewed and reattested in perfection of all its parts, in solid and flawless unity, whole and indissoluble. Scarcely one or two of all Byron's poems will stand any such test for a moment: and his enemies, it must again be explained, are those eyeless and earless panegyrists who will not let us overlook this infirmity. It is to Byron and not to Tennyson that Mr. Austin has proved himself an enemy; the enemies of Tennyson are critics of another class: they are those of his own household. They are not the men who bring against the sweetest

and the noblest examples[18] of his lyric work their charges of
pettiness or tameness, contraction or inadequacy; who taste a
savour of corruption in "The Sisters" or a savour of effeminacy in
"Boadicea." They are the men who couple "In Memoriam" with
the Psalms of David as a work akin to these in scope and in
effect; who compare the dramatic skill and subtle power to sound
the depths of the human spirit displayed in "Maud" with the like
display of these gifts in Hamlet and Othello. They are the men
who would set his ode on the death of Wellington above Shelley's
lines on the death of Napoleon, his "Charge of the Light Brigade"
beside Campbell's "Battle of the Baltic" or Drayton's "Battle of
Agincourt," the very poem whose model it follows afar off with
such halting and unequal steps. They are the men who find in
his collection of Arthurian idyls,—the Morte d'Albert as it might
perhaps be more properly called, after the princely type to which
(as he tells us with just pride) the poet has been fortunate enough
to make his central figure so successfully conform,—an epic poem
of profound and exalted morality. Upon this moral question I
shall take leave to intercalate a few words. It does not appear to
me that on the whole I need stand in fear of misapprehension or
misrepresentation on one charge at least—that of envious or
grudging reluctance to applaud the giver of any good gift for
which all receivers should be glad to return thanks. I am not
aware—but it is possible that this too may be an instance of a
man's blindness to his own defects—of having by any overt or
covert demonstration of so vile a spirit exposed my name to be
classed with the names, whether forged or genuine, of the rancorous and reptile crew of poeticules who decompose into critic-
asters; I do not remember to have ever as yet been driven by
despair or hunger or malevolence to take up the trade of throwing dirt in the dark; nor am I conscious, at sight of my superiors,
of an instant impulse to revile them. My first instinct, in such a
case, is not the instinct of backbiting; I have even felt at such
times some moderate sense of delight and admiration, and some
slight pleasure in the attempt to express it loyally by such modest
thanksgiving as I might. I hold myself therefore free to say what
I think on this matter without fear of being taxed with the motives
of a currish malignant. It seems to me that the moral tone of the

Arthurian story has been on the whole lowered and degraded by Mr. Tennyson's mode of treatment. Wishing to make his central figure the noble and perfect symbol of an ideal man, he has removed not merely the excuse but the explanation of the fatal and tragic loves of Launcelot and Guenevere. The hinge of the whole legend of the Round Table, from its first glory to its final fall, is the incestuous birth of Mordred from the connexion of Arthur with his half-sister, unknowing and unknown; as surely as the hinge of the Oresteia from first to last is the sacrifice at Aulis. From the immolation of Iphigenia springs the wrath of Clytæmnestra, with[19] all its train of evils ensuing;[20] from the sin of Arthur's youth proceeds the ruin of his reign and realm through the falsehood of his wife, a wife unloving and unloved. Remove in either case the plea which leaves the heroine less sinned against indeed than sinning, but yet not too base for tragic compassion and interest, and there remains merely the presentation of a vulgar adulteress. From the background of the one story the ignoble figure of Ægisthus starts into the foreground, and we see in place of the terrible and patient mother, perilous and piteous as a lioness bereaved, the congenial harlot of a coward and traitor. A poet undertaking to rewrite the Agamemnon[21] who should open his poem with some scene of dalliance or conspiracy between Ægisthus and Clytæmnestra[22] and proceed to make of their common household intrigue the mainspring of his plan, would not more deform the design[23] and lower the keynote of the Æschylean drama[24] than Mr. Tennyson has lowered the note and deformed the outline of the Arthurian story[25] by reducing Arthur to the level of a wittol, Guenevere to the level of a woman of intrigue, and Launcelot to the level of a "co-respondent." Treated as he has treated it, the story is rather a case for the divorce-court than for poetry. At the utmost it might serve the recent censor of his countrymen, the champion of morals so dear to President Thiers and the virtuous journalist who draws a contrast in favour of his chastity between him and other French or English authors, for a new study of the worn and wearisome old topic of domestic intrigue; but such "camelias" should be left to blow in the common hotbeds of the lower kind of novelist. Adultery must be tragic and exceptional to afford stuff for art to work upon; and the debased preference of Mr. Tennyson's heroine for a lover so much beneath her noble and faithful husband is as mean an instance as any day can show in its newspaper reports of a common woman's common sin. In the old story, the king, with the doom denounced in the beginning by Merlin hanging over all his toils and triumphs as a tragic shadow, stands apart in no undignified patience to await the end in its own good time of all his work and glory, with no eye for the pain and passion of the woman who sits beside him as queen rather than as wife. Such a figure is not unfit for the centre of a tragic action; it is neither ignoble nor inconceivable; but the besotted blindness of Mr. Tennyson's "blameless king" to the treason of a woman who has had the first and last of his love and the whole devotion of his blameless life is nothing more or less than pitiful and ridiculous. All the studious care and exquisite eloquence of the poet can throw no genuine halo round the sprouting brows of a royal husband who remains to the very last the one man in his kingdom insensible of his disgrace. The unclean taunt of the hateful Vivien is simply the expression in vile language of an undeniable truth; such a man as this king is indeed hardly "man at all"; either fool or coward he must surely be. Thus it is that by the very excision of what may have seemed in his eyes a moral blemish Mr. Tennyson has blemished the whole story; by the very exaltation of his hero as something more than man he has left him in the end something less. The keystone of the whole building is removed, and in place of a tragic house of song where even sin had all the dignity and beauty that sin can retain, and without which it can afford no fit material for tragedy, we find an incongruous edifice of tradition and invention where even virtue is made to seem either imbecile or vile. The story as it stood of old had in it something almost of Hellenic dignity and significance; in it as in the great Greek legends we could trace from a seemingly small root of evil the birth and growth of a calamitous fate, not sent by mere malevolence of heaven, yet in its awful weight and mystery of darkness apparently out of all due retributive proportion to the careless sin or folly of presumptuous weakness which first incurred its infliction; so that by mere hasty resistance and return of violence for violence a noble man may unwittingly bring on himself and all his house the curse denounced on parricide, by mere casual indulgence of light love and passing wantonness a hero king may unknowingly bring on himself and all his kingdom the doom imposed on incest. This presence and imminence of Ate inevitable as invisible throughout the tragic course of action can alone confer on such a story the proper significance and the necessary dignity:[26] without it the action would want meaning and the passion would want nobility; with it, we may hear in the high funereal homily which concludes as with dirge-music the great old book of Sir Thomas Mallory some echo not utterly unworthy of that supreme lament of wondering and wailing spirits—

$$\pi o\hat{\imath} \ \delta\hat{\eta}\tau a \ \kappa\rho a\nu\epsilon\hat{\imath}, \ \pi o\hat{\imath} \ \kappa a\tau a\lambda\acute{\eta}\xi\epsilon\iota$$
$$\mu\epsilon\tau a\kappa o\iota\mu\iota\sigma\theta\grave{\epsilon}\nu \ \mu\acute{\epsilon}\nu o\varsigma \ \ddot{a}\tau\eta\varsigma;$$

The fatal consequence or corollary of this original flaw in his scheme is that the modern poet has been obliged to degrade all the other figures of the legend in order to bring them into due harmony with the degraded figures of Arthur and Guenevere. The courteous and loyal Gawain of the old romancers, already deformed and maligned in the version of Mallory himself, is here a vulgar traitor; the benignant Lady of the Lake, foster-mother of Launcelot, redeemer and comforter of Pelleas, becomes the very vilest figure in all that cycle of more or less symbolic agents and patients which[27] Mr. Tennyson has set revolving round the figure of his central wittol. I certainly do not share the objection of the virtuous journalist to the presentation in art of an unchaste woman; but I certainly desire that the creature presented should retain some trace of human or if need be of devilish dignity. The Vivien of Mr. Tennyson's idyl seems to me, to speak frankly, about the most base and repulsive person ever set forth in serious literature. Her impurity is actually eclipsed by her incredible and incomparable vulgarity—("O ay," said Vivien,[28] "*that were likely too*"). She is such a sordid creature as plucks men passing by the sleeve. I am of course aware that this figure appears the very type and model of a beautiful and fearful temptress of the flesh, the very embodied and ennobled ideal of danger and desire, in the chaster eyes of the virtuous journalist who grows sick with horror and disgust at the license of other French and English writers; but I have yet to find the French or English contemporary poem containing a passage that can be matched against the loathsome dialogue in which Merlin and Vivien discuss the nightly transgressions against chastity, within doors and without, of the various knights of Arthur's court. I do not remember that any modern poet whose fame has been assailed on the score of sensual immorality—say for instance the author of "Mademoiselle de Maupin" or the author of the "Fleurs du Mal"—has ever devoted an elaborate poem to describing the erotic fluctuations and vacillations of a dotard under the moral and physical manipulation of a prostitute. The conversation of Vivien is exactly described in the poet's own phrase—it is "as the poached filth that floods the middle street." Nothing like it can be cited from the verse which embodies other poetic personations of unchaste women. From the Cleopatra of Shakespeare and the Dalilah of Milton to the Phraxanor of Wells, a figure worthy to be ranked not far in design below the highest of theirs, we may pass without fear of finding any such pollution. Those heroines of sin are evil, but noble in their evil way; it is the utterly ignoble quality of Vivien which makes her so unspeakably repulsive and unfit for artistic treatment. "Smiling saucily," she is simply a subject for the police-court. The "Femmes Damnées" of Baudelaire may be worthier of hell-fire than a common harlot like this, but that side of their passion which would render them amenable to the notice of the nearest station is not what is kept before us throughout that condemned poem; it is an infinite perverse refinement, an infinite reverse aspiration, "the end of which things is death"; and from the barren places of unsexed desire the tragic lyrist points them at last along their downward way to the land of sleepless winds and scourging storms, where the shadows of things perverted shall toss and turn for ever in a Dantesque cycle and agony of changeless change:[29] a lyric close of bitter tempest and deep wide music of lost souls, not inaptly described by M. Asselineau as a "fulgurant" harmony after the fashion of Beethoven. The slight sketch in eight lines of Matha in "Ratbert" resumes all the imaginable horror and loveliness of a wicked and beautiful woman; but Hugo does not make her open her lips to let out the foul talk or the "saucy" smile of the common street. "La blonde

fauve," all but naked among the piled-up roses, with feet dabbled
in blood, and the laughter of hell itself on her rose-red mouth, is
as horrible as any proper object of art can be; but she is not vile
and intolerable as Vivien. I do not fear or hesitate to say on this
occasion what I think and have always thought on this matter;
for I trust to have shown before now that the poet in the sunshine
of whose noble genius the men of my generation grew up and
took delight has no more ardent or more loyal admirer than myself among the herd of imitative parasites and thievish satellites
who grovel at his heels; that I need feel no apprehension of being
placed "in the rank of verminous fellows" who let themselves
out to lie for hatred or for hire—"qui quæstum non corporis sed
animi sui faciunt," as Major Dalgetty might have defined them.
Among these obscene vermin I do not hold myself liable to be
classed; though I may be unworthy to express, however capable
of feeling, the same abhorrence as the Quarterly reviewer of
"Vivien" for the exhibition of the libidinous infirmity of unvener-
able age. But these are not the grounds on which Mr. Austin
objects to the ethical tendency of Mr. Tennyson's poetry. His
complaint against all those of his countrymen who spend their
time in writing verse is that their verse is devoted to the worship
of "woman, woman, woman, woman." He "hardly likes to own
sex with" a man who devotes his life to the love of a woman, and
is ready to lay down his life and to sacrifice his soul for the chance
of preserving her reputation. It is probable that the reluctance
would be cordially reciprocated. A writer about as much beneath
Mr. Austin as Mr. Austin is beneath the main objects of his attack
has charged certain poetry of the present day with constant and
distasteful recurrence of devotion to "some person of the other
sex." It is at least significant that this person should have come
forward, for once under his own name, to vindicate the moral
worth of Petronius Arbiter; a writer, I believe, whose especial
weakness (as exhibited in the characters of his book) was not a
"hankering" after persons "of the other sex." It is as well to
remember where we may be when we find ourselves in the company of these anti-sexual moralists.

Effeminate therefore I suppose the modern poetry of England
must be content to remain; but there is a poet alive of now ac-

knowledged eminence, not hitherto assailed on this hand, about whom the masked or barefaced critics of the minute are not by any means of one mind—if mind we are to call the organ which forms and produces their opinions. To me it seems that the truth for good and evil has never yet been spoken about Walt Whitman. There are in him two distinct men of most inharmonious kinds; a poet and a formalist. Of the poet I have before now done the best I could to express, whether in verse or prose, my ardent and sympathetic admiration. Of the formalist I shall here say what I think; showing why (for example) I cannot for my own part share in full the fiery partisanship of such thoughtful and eloquent disciples as Mr. Rossetti and Dr. Burroughs. It is from no love of foolish paradox that I have chosen the word "formalist" to express my sense of the radical fault in the noble genius of Whitman. For truly no scholar and servant of the past, reared on academic tradition under the wing of old-world culture, was ever more closely bound in with his own theories, more rigidly regulated by his own formularies, than this poet of new life and limitless democracy. Not Pope, not Boileau, was more fatally a formalist than Whitman; only Whitman is a poet of a greater nature than they. It is simply that these undigested formulas which choke by fits the free passage of his genius are to us less familiar than theirs; less real or less evident they are not. Throughout his great book, now of late so nobly completed, you can always tell at first hearing whether it be the poet who speaks or the formalist. Sometimes in the course of two lines the note is changed, either by the collapse of the poet's voice into the tuneless twang of the formalist, or by the sudden break and rise of released music from the formalist's droning note into the clear sincere harmonies of the poet. Sometimes for one whole division of the work either the formalist intones throughout as to order, or the poet sings high and true and strong without default from end to end. It is of no matter whatever, though both disciples and detractors appear to assume that it must be at least in each other's eyes, whether the subject treated be conventionally high or low, pleasant or unpleasant. At once and without fail you can hear whether the utterance of the subject be right or wrong; this is the one thing needful,[30] but then this one thing is needful indeed. Disciples and detractors alike seem to assume that if you object to certain work of Whitman's it must be because you object to his choice of topic and would object equally to any man's choice or treatment of it; if you approve, it must be that you approve of the choice of topic and would approve equally of any poem that should start for the same end and run on the same lines. It is not so in the least. Let a man come forward as does Whitman with prelude of promise that he is about to sing and celebrate certain things, fair or foul, great or small, these being as good stuff for song and celebration as other things, we wait, admitting that, to hear if he will indeed celebrate and sing them. If he does, and does it well and duly, there is an end; *solvitur ambulando;* the matter is settled once for all by the invaluable and indispensable proof of the pudding. Now whenever the pure poet in Whitman speaks, it is settled by that proof in his favour; whenever the mere theorist in him speaks, it is settled by the same proof against him. What comes forth out of the abundance of his heart rises at once from that high heart to the lips on which its thoughts take fire, and the music which rolls from them rings true as fine gold and perfect; what comes forth by the dictation of doctrinal theory serves only to twist aside his hand and make the written notes run foolishly awry. What he says is well said when he speaks as of himself and because he cannot choose but speak; whether he speak of a small bird's loss or a great man's death, of a nation rising for battle or a child going forth in the morning. What he says is not well said when he speaks not as though he must but as though he ought; as though it behoved one who would be the poet of American democracy to do this thing or to be that thing[31] if the duties of that office were to be properly fulfilled, the tenets of that religion worthily delivered. Never before was high poetry so puddled and adulterated with mere doctrine in its crudest form. Never was there less assimilation of the lower dogmatic with the higher prophetic element. It so happens that the present writer (*si quid id est*) is, as far as he knows, entirely at one with Whitman on general matters not less than on political; if there be in Whitman's works any opinion expressed on outward and social or inward and spiritual subjects which would clash or contend with his own, or with which he would feel his own to be incapable of concord or sympathy, he has yet to find the passage in which that opinion is embodied. To him the views of life and of death set forth by Whitman appear thoroughly acceptable and noble, perfectly credible and sane. It is certainly therefore from no prejudice against the doctrines delivered that he objects in any case to the delivery of them. What he objects—to take two small instances— is that it is one thing to sing the song of all trades, and quite another thing to tumble down together the names of all possible crafts and implements in one unsorted heap; to sing the song of all countries is not simply to fling out on the page at random in one howling mass the titles of all divisions of the earth, and so leave them. At this rate, to sing the song of the language it should suffice to bellow out backwards and forwards the twenty-four letters of the alphabet. And this folly is deliberately done by a great writer, and ingeniously defended by able writers, alike in good faith, and alike in blind bondage to mere dogmatic theory, to the mere formation of foregone opinion. They cannot see that formalism need not by any means be identical with tradition: they cannot see that because theories of the present are not in-herited they do not on that account become more proper than were theories of the past to suffice of themselves for poetic or prophetic speech. Whether you have to deliver an old or a brand-new creed, alike in either case you must first insure that it be delivered well; for in neither will it suffice you to deliver it simply in good faith and good intent. The poet of democracy must sing all things alike? let him sing them then, whether in rhyme or not is no matter,* but in rhythm he must needs sing them. What is

---

* In Dr. Burroughs' excellent little book there is a fault common to almost all champions of his great friend; they will treat Whitman as "Athanasius contra mundum:" they will assume that if he be right all other poets must be wrong; and if this intimation were confined to America there might be some plausible reason to admit it; but if we pass beyond and have to choose between Whitman and the world, we must regretfully drop the "Leaves of Grass" and retain at least for example the "Légende des Siècles." As to this matter of rhythm and rhyme, prose and verse, I find in this little essay some things which out of pure regard and sympathy I could wish away, and consigned to the more congenial page of some tenth-rate poeticule worn out with failure after failure, and now squat in his hole like the tailless fox he is, curled up to snarl and whimper beneath the inaccessible vine of song. Let me suggest that it may *not* be observed in the grand literary relics of nations that their best poetry has always, or has ever, adopted essentially the prose

true of all poets is among them all most markedly true of Whitman, that his manner and his matter grow together; that where you catch a note of discord there you will find something wrong inly, the natural source of that outer wrongdoing; wherever you catch a note of good music you will surely find that it came whence only it could come, from some true root of music in the thought or thing spoken. There never was and will never be a poet who had verbal harmony and nothing else; if there was in him no inner depth or strength or truth, then that which men took for music in his mere speech was no such thing as music.

By far the finest and truest thing yet said of Walt Whitman has been said by himself, and said worthily of a great man. "I perceive in clear moments," he said to his friend Dr. Burroughs, "that my work is not the accomplishment of perfections, but destined, I hope, always to arouse an unquenchable feeling and ardour for them." A hope, surely, as well grounded as it is noble. But it is in those parts of his work which most arouse this feeling and this ardour that we find him nearest that accomplishment. At such times his speech has a majestic harmony which hurts us by

---

form, preserving interior rhythm only. I do not "ask dulcet rhymes from" Whitman; I far prefer his rhythms to any merely "dulcet metres"; I would have him in nowise other than he is; but I certainly do not wish to see his form or style reproduced at second hand[32] by a school of disciples with less deep and exalted sense of rhythm. As to rhyme, there is some rhymed verse that holds more music, carries more weight, flies higher and wider in equal scope of sense and sound, than all but the highest human speech has ever done,[33] and would have done no more, as no verse has done more, had it been unrhymed; witness the song of the Earth from Shelley's "Prometheus Unbound." Do as well without rhyme if you can, or do as well with rhyme, it is of no moment whatever; a thing not noticeable or perceptible except by pedants and sciolists; in either case your triumph will be equal. In a precious and memorable excerpt given by Dr. Burroughs from some article in the *North American Review,* the writer, a German by his name, after much gabble against prosody, observes with triumph as a final instance of the progress of language that *"the spiritualizing and enfranchising influence* of Christianity transformed Greek into an accentuated language." The present poets of Greece,[34] I presume, know better than to waste their genius on the same ridiculous elaborations of corresponsive metre which occupied the pagan and benighted intellects of Æschylus and Pindar. I have heard before now of many deliverances wrought by Christianity; but I had never yet perceived that among the most remarkable of these—"an outward and visible sign of an inward and spiritual grace"—was to be reckoned the transformation of the language spoken under Pericles into the language spoken under King Otho and King George.

no imperfection; his music then is absolutely great and good. It is when he is thinking of his part, of the duties and properties of a representative poet, an official democrat, that the strength forsakes his hand and the music ceases at his lips. It is then that he sets himself to define what books, and to what purpose, the scriptural code of democracy must accept and reject; to determine, Pope himself and council in one, what shall be the canons and articles of the church, which except a democrat do keep whole and undefiled, without doubt he shall perish everlastingly. With more than Athanasian assurance, with more than Calvinistic rigour, it is then that he pronounces what things are democratic and of good report, what things are feudal and of evil report, in all past literature of the world. There is much in these canonical decrees that is consonant with truth and reason; there is not a little that is simply the babbling of a preacher made drunk with his own doctrine. For instance, we find that "the Democratic requirements" substantially and curiously fulfilled in the best Spanish literature are not only not fulfilled in the best English literature, but are insulted in every page. After this it appears to us that in common consistency the best remaining type of actual democracy in Europe here must be sought among French or Austrian Legitimists, if not on some imperial Russian or German throne. But Shakespeare is not only "the tally of Feudalism," he is "incarnated, uncompromising Feudalism, in[35] literature." Now Shakespeare has doubtless done work which is purely aristocratic in tone. The supreme embodiment in poetic form of the aristocratic idea is "Coriolanus." I cannot at all accept the very good special pleading of M. François-Victor Hugo against this the natural view of that great tragedy. Whether we like it or not, the fact seems to me undeniable that Shakespeare has here used all his art and might to subdue the many to the one, to degrade the figure of the people, to enhance and exalt the figure of the people's enemy. Even here, though, he has not done as in Whitman's view he does always; he has not left without shades the radiant figure, he has not left the sombre figure without lights; there are blemishes here and there on the towering glory of Coriolanus, redeeming points now and then in the grovelling ignominy of the commons. But what if there were none? Is this play the keynote of Shakespeare's mind,

the keystone of his work? If the word Democracy mean anything
—and to Whitman it means much—beyond the mere profession
of a certain creed, the mere iteration of a certain shibboleth; if
it signify first the cyclic life and truth of equal and various humanity, and secondly the form of principles and relations, the code
of duties and of rights, by which alone adult society can walk
straight; surely in the first and greatest sense there has never
been and never can be a book so infinitely democratic as the
Plays of Shakespeare.

These among others are reasons why I think it foolish to talk
of Whitman as the probable founder of a future school of poetry
unlike any other in matter as in style. He has many of the qualities
of a reformer; he has perhaps none of the qualities of a founder.
For one thing, he is far too didactic to be typical; the prophet in
him too frequently subsides into the lecturer. He is not one of
the everlasting models; but as an original and individual poet, it
is at his best hardly possible to overrate him; as an informing and
reforming element, it is absolutely impossible. Never did a country
need more than America such an influence as his. We may understand and even approve his reproachful and scornful fear of the
overweening "British element" when we see what it has hitherto
signified in the literature of his country. Once as yet, and once
only, has there sounded out of it all one pure note of original song
—worth singing, and echoed from the singing of no other man;
a note of song neither wide nor deep, but utterly true, rich, clear,
and native to the singer; the short exquisite music, subtle and
simple and sombre and sweet, of Edgar Poe. All the rest that is
not of mocking-birds is of corncrakes, varied but at best for an
instant by some scant-winded twitter of linnet or of wren.

We have[36] been looking up too long from the microscope;
it is time to look in again and take note of the subject. We find
indeed one American name on which our weekly critics cluster
in swarms of praise; one poet whom they who agree in nothing
else but hate agree to love and laud as king of American verse;
who has sung, they tell us, a song at last truly national and truly
noble. The singer is Mr. Lowell; but the song is none of the
Biglow Papers, where the humours could not but tickle while
the discords made us wince; we laughed, with ears yet flayed

and teeth still on edge. The song so preferable to any "Drum-Tap" of Whitman's was a Thanksgiving Ode of wooden verse sawn into unequal planks and tagged incongruously with tuneless bells of rhyme torn from the author's late professional cap. It was modelled on the chaotic songs of ceremony done to order on state occasions by our laureates of the Restoration and Revolution; preferable in this alone, that the modern author had the grace not to call it Pindaric: which in the sense of Whitehall, not of Thebes, it was; being cut into verses uneven, misshapen, irregular, and irresponsive. As a speech it might have passed muster on the platform; as a song it gave out no sound but such as of the platform's wood. Nor indeed could it; for while it had something of thought and more of eloquence, there was within it no breath or pulse of the thing called poetry. This gracious chant among others has been much belauded—incomparably beyond any praise given in any such quarter to Whitman's deathless hymn of death—by a writer on poetry whom Mr. Austin has reviled with as much acrimony as if he were instead a poet; calling his poor fellow-critic "an ignorant and presumptuous scribbler, wholly unentitled to give an opinion on poetry at all." Far be it from me this time to dispute the perfect justice of the verdict; but I had some hope till now that there might be truth in the proverb, "Hawks do not pyke out hawks' een." It is painful for the naturalist to be compelled to register in his note-book the fact that there is none. It is sad that the hymnologist, to whom this fact may be yet unknown, should be obliged, after citing the peaceful example of the aviary, to reiterate the lesson that 'tis a shameful sight when critics of one progeny fall out and chide and fight.* Really they should remember that their office is to instruct; and if so, surely not by precept alone. If the monitors of the poetic school go together by the ears in this way in sight of all forms at

---

* I cannot help calling just now to mind an epigram—very rude, after the fashion of the time, but here certainly not impertinent but pertinent—cited by Boswell on a quarrel between two "beaux"; the second stanza runs thus, with one word altered of necessity, as that quarrel was not on poetry but on religion:—

> "Peace, coxcombs, peace! and both agree;
>   A., kiss thy empty brother;
> The Muses love a foe like thee,
>   But dread a friend like t'other."

once, what can be expected of those whom they were appointed
(though God only knows by whom) to direct and correct at need?
The dirtiest little sneak on the dunce's seat may be encouraged to
play some blackguard's trick on better boys behind their backs, and
so oblige some one who had no thought of bullying or of noticing
such a cur to kick him out into the yard and cleanse the old school
of scandalous rubbish. And what may not one of the headmasters[37]
(there are more than one in this school), at their next quarterly
visitation, say to such a couple of monitors as this?

> Their little hands were never made
> To tear each other's eyes.

Their little hands—can it be necessary to remind them?—were
made to throw dirt and stones with impunity at passers-by of a
different kind. This is their usual business, and they do it with a
will; though (to drop metaphor for a while[38]) we may concede
that English reviewers—and among them the reviewer of the
"Spectator"—have not always been unready to do accurate justice
to the genuine worth of new American writers; among much poor
patchwork of comic and serious stuff, which shared their welcome
and diminished its worth, they have yet found some fit word of
praise for the true pathos of Bret Harte, the true passion of
Joaquin Miller. But the men really and naturally dear to them
are the literators of Boston; truly, and in no good sense, the school
of New England—Britannia pejor:[39] a land of dissonant re-
verberations and distorted reflections from our own.*[40] This preference for the province of reflex poets and echoing philosophers
came to a climax of expression in the transcendant remark that

---

* Not that the British worshipper gets much tolerance for his countrymen in
return. In an eloquent essay on the insolence of Englishmen towards Americans, for
which doubtless there are but too good grounds, Mr. Lowell shows himself as sore
as a whipped cutpurse of the days "ere carts had lost their tails" under the vulgar
imputation of vulgarity. It is doubtless a very gross charge, and one often flung at
Americans by English lackeys and bullies of the vulgarest order. Is there ever any
ground for it discernible in the dainty culture of overbred letters which, as we hear,
distinguishes New England? I remember to have read a passage from certain notes
of travel in Italy published by an eminent and eloquent writer—that I could but
remember his name and grace my page with it!—who after some just remarks on
Byron's absurd and famous description of a waterfall, proceeds to observe that
Milton was the only poet who ever made real poetry out of a cataract—"AND
THAT WAS IN HIS EYE."

Mr. Lowell had in one critical essay so taken Mr. Carlyle to pieces[41] that it would seem impossible ever to put him together again. Under the stroke of that recollected sentence, the staggered spirit of a sane man who desires to retain his sanity can but pause and reflect on what Mr. Ruskin, if I rightly remember, has somewhere said, that ever since Mr. Carlyle began to write you can tell by the reflex action of his genius the nobler from the ignobler of his contemporaries; as ever having won the most of reverence and praise from the most honourable among these, and (what is perhaps as sure a warrant of sovereign worth) from the most despicable among them the most of abhorrence and abuse.

A notable example of this latter sort was not long since (in his "Fors Clavigera") selected and chastised by Mr. Ruskin himself with a few strokes of such a lash as might thenceforward, one would think, have secured silence at least, if neither penitence nor shame, on the part of the offender. This person, whose abuse of Mr. Carlyle he justly described[42] as matchless "in its platitudinous obliquity," was cited by the name of one Buchanan—

$$\text{ὅστις ποτ' ἐστίν, εἰ τόδ' αὐ-}$$
$$\text{τῷ φίλον κεκλημένῳ—}$$

but whether by his right name or another, who shall say? for the god of song himself had not more names or addresses. Now yachting among the Scottish (not English) Hebrides; now wrestling with fleshly sin (like his countryman Holy Willie) in "a great city of civilization"; now absorbed in studious emulation of the Persæ of Æschylus or the "enormously fine" work of "the tremendous creature" Dante;* now descending from the familiar heights of men whose praise he knows so well how to sing, for the not less noble purpose of crushing a school of poetic sensualists whose works are "wearing to the brain"; now "walking down the streets" and watching "harlots stare from the shop-windows," while "in the broad day a dozen hands offer him indecent prints"; now "beguiling many an hour, when snug at anchor in some

---

* Lest it should seem impossible that these and the like could be the actual expressions of any articulate creature, I have invariably in such a context marked as quotations only the exact words of this unutterable author, either as I find them cited by others or as they fall under my own eye in glancing among his essays. More trouble than this I am not disposed to take with him.

lovely Highland loch, with the inimitable, yet questionable, pictures of Parisian life left by Paul de Kock"; landsman and seaman, Londoner and Scotchman, Delian and Patarene Buchanan. How should one address him?

> Matutine pater, seu Jane libentiùs audis?

As Janus rather, one would think, being so in all men's sight a natural son of the double-faced divinity. Yet it might be well for the son of Janus if he had read and remembered in time the inscription on the statue of another divine person, before taking his name in vain as a word wherewith to revile men born in the ordinary way of the flesh:—

> Youngsters! who write false names, and slink
> behind
> The honest garden-god to hide yourselves,
> Beware!

In vain would I try to play the part of a prologuizer before this latest rival of the Hellenic dramatists, who sings from the height of "mystic realism," not with notes echoed from a Grecian strain, but as a Greek poet himself might have sung, in "massive grandeur of style," of a great contemporary event. He alone is fit, in Euripidean fashion, to prologuize for himself.

> Πολὺs[43] μὲν ἐν γραφαῖσι κοὐκ ἀνώνυμος
> ψεύστης κέκλημαι Σκότιος,* ἄστεως τ᾽ ἔσω,
> ὅσοι τε πόντου τερμόνων τ᾽ Ἀτλαντικῶν
> ναίουσιν ἔξω σκάφεσι νησιωτικοῖς,
> τοὺς μὲν τρέφοντας θώψ ἀπὸ γλώσσης σέβω,
> ὅσοι δ᾽ ἀποπτύουσί μ᾽ ἐμπίπτω λαθών.†

He has often written, it seems, under false or assumed names; always doubtless "with the best of all motives," that which induced his friends in his absence to alter an article abusive of his betters and suppress the name which would otherwise have signed it, that of saving the writer from persecution and letting his

---

* For the occasions on which the word σκότιος is to be spelt with a capital Σ, the student should consult the last-century glossaries of Lauder and Macpherson.

† There are other readings of the two last lines:

> τοὺς δεσπότας μὲν δουλιᾷ σαίνω φρενί,
> ὅσοι δὲ μ᾽ ἀγνοοῦσιν (Cod. Var. ὅσοισι δ᾽ εἰμ᾽ ἄγνωτος) κ. τ. λ.

charges stand on their own merits; and this simple and very
natural precaution has singularly enough exposed his fair fame
to "the inventions of cowards"—a form of attack naturally intolerable though contemptible to this polyonymous moralist. He
was not used to it; in the cradle where his genius had been hatched
he could remember no taint of such nastiness. Other friends than
such had fostered into maturity the genius that now lightens far
and wide the fields of poetry and criticism. All things must have
their beginnings; and there were those who watched with prophetic hope the beginnings of Mr. Buchanan; who tended the rosy
and lisping infancy of his genius with a care for its comfort and
cleanliness not unworthy the nurse of Orestes; and took indeed
much the same pains to keep it sweet and neat under the eye and
nose of the public as those on which the good woman dwelt with
such pathetic minuteness of recollection in after years. The babe
may not always have been discreet;

$$\nu\acute{\epsilon}\alpha \ \delta\grave{\epsilon} \ \nu\eta\delta\grave{\upsilon}s \ \alpha\grave{\upsilon}\tau\acute{\alpha}\rho\kappa\eta s \ \tau\acute{\epsilon}\kappa\nu\omega\nu\cdot$$

and there were others who found its swaddling clothes not invariably in such condition as to dispense with the services of the
"fuller";

$$\gamma\nu\alpha\phi\epsilon\grave{\upsilon}s \ \tau\rho\phi\epsilon\acute{\upsilon}s \ \tau\epsilon \ \tau\alpha\grave{\upsilon}\tau\grave{\upsilon}\nu^{44} \ \epsilon\grave{\iota}\chi\acute{\epsilon}\tau\eta\nu \ \tau\acute{\epsilon}\lambda\omicron s.$$

In effect[45] there were those who found the woes and devotions
of Doll Tearsheet or Nell Nameless as set forth in the lyric verse
of Mr. Buchanan calculated rather to turn the stomach than to
melt the heart. But in spite of these exceptional tastes the nursing
journals, it should seem, abated no jot of heart or hope for their
nursling.

> Petit poisson deviendra grand
> Pourvu que Dieu lui prête vie.

Petit bonhomme will not, it appears. The tadpole poet will never
grow into anything bigger than a frog; not though in that stage of
development he should puff and blow himself till he bursts with
windy adulation at the heels of the laurelled ox.

When some time since a passing notice was bestowed by
writers of another sort on Mr. Buchanan's dramatic performance
in the part of Thomas Maitland, it was observed with very just

indignation by a literary ally that Mr. Rossetti was not ashamed
to avow in the face of heaven and the press his utter ignorance of
the writings of that poet—or perhaps we should say of those
poets. The loss was too certainly his own. It is no light thing for
a man who has any interest in the poetic production of his time to
be ignorant of works which have won from the critic who[46] of all
others must be most competent to speak on the subject with the
authority of the most intimate acquaintance, such eloquence of
praise as has deservedly been lavished on Mr. Buchanan. A living
critic of no less note in the world of letters than himself has drawn
public attention to the deep and delicate beauties of his work; to
"the intense loving tenderness of the coarse woman Nell towards
her brutal paramour, the exquisite delicacy and fine spiritual
vision of the old village schoolmaster," &c. &c. This pathetic
tribute to the poet Buchanan was paid by no less a person than
Buchanan the critic. Its effect is heightened by comparison with
the just but rigid severity of that writer's verdict on other men—
on the "gross" work of Shakespeare, the "brutal" work of Carlyle,
the "sickening and peculiar" work of Thackeray, the "wooden-
headed," "hectic," and "hysterical" qualities which are severally
notable and condemnable in the work of Landor, of Keats, and of
Shelley. In like manner his condemnation of contemporary impurities is thrown into fuller relief by his tribute to the moral sincerity
of Petronius and the "singular purity" of Ben Jonson. For once
I have the honour and pleasure to agree with him; I find the
"purity" of the author of "Bartholomew Fair" a very "singular"
sort of purity indeed. There is however another play of that great
writer's, which, though it might be commended by his well-wishers
to the special study of Mr. Buchanan, I can hardly suppose to be
the favourite work which has raised the old poet so high in his
esteem. In this play Jonson has traced with his bitterest fidelity the
career of a "gentleman parcel-poet," one Laberius Crispinus, whose
life is spent in the struggle to make his way among his betters by
a happy alternation and admixture of calumny with servility; one
who will fasten himself uninvited on the acquaintance of a superior with fulsome and obtrusive ostentation of good-will; inflict
upon his passive and reluctant victim the recitation of his verses
in a public place; offer him friendship and alliance against all

other poets, so as "to lift the best of them out of favour"; protest
to him, "Do but taste me once, if I do know myself and my own
virtues truly, thou wilt not make that esteem of Varius, or Virgil,
or Tibullus, or any of 'em indeed, as now in thy ignorance thou
dost; which I am content to forgive; I would fain see which of
these could pen more verses in a day or with more facility than
I." After this, it need hardly be added that the dog returns to his
vomit, and has in the end to be restrained by authority from vent-
ing "divers and sundry calumnies" against the victim aforesaid
"or any other eminent man transcending him in merit, whom his
envy shall find cause to work upon, either for that, or for keeping
himself in better acquaintance, or enjoying better friends"; and
the play is aptly wound up by his public exposure and ignominious
punishment. The title of this admirable comedy is "The Poetaster;
or, His Arraignment"; and the prologue is spoken by Envy.

It is really to be regretted that the new fashion of self-criticism
should never have been set till now. How much petty trouble, how
many paltry wrangles and provocations, what endless warfare of the
cranes and pigmies might have been prevented—and by how
simple a remedy! How valuable would the applauding comments
of other great poets on their own work have been to us for all
time! All students of poetry must lament that it did not occur to
Milton for example to express in public his admiration of "Paradise Lost." It might have helped to support the reputation of that
poem against the severe sentence passed by Mr. Buchanan on its
frequently flat and prosaic quality. And, like all truly great dis-
coveries, this one looks so easy now we have it before us, that we
cannot but wonder it was reserved for Mr. Buchanan to make: we
cannot but feel it singular that Mr. Tennyson should never have
thought fit to call our attention in person to the beauties of
"Maud"; that Mr. Browning should never have come forward,
"motley on back and pointing-pole in hand," to bid us remark the
value of "The Ring and the Book"; that Mr. Arnold should have
left to others the task of praising his "Thyrsis" and "Empedocles."
The last-named poet might otherwise have held his own even
against the imputation of writing "mere prose" which now he
shares with Milton: so sharp is the critical judgment, so high the
critical standard, of the author of "The Book of Orm."

However, even in the face of the rebuke so deservedly incurred by the avowal of Mr. Rossetti's gross and deplorable ignorance of that and other great works from the same hand, I am bound in honesty to admit that my own studies in that line are hardly much less limited. I cannot profess to have read any book of Mr. Buchanan's; for aught I know, they may deserve all his praises; it is neither my business nor my desire to decide. But sundry of his contributions in verse and prose to various magazines and newspapers I have looked through or glanced over—not, I trust, without profit; not, I know, without amusement. From these casual sources I have gathered—as he who runs may gather—not a little information on no unimportant matters of critical and autobiographical interest. With the kindliest forethought, the most judicious care to anticipate the anxious researches of a late posterity, Mr. Buchanan has once and again poured out his personal confidences into the sympathetic bosom of the nursing journals. He is resolved that his country shall not always have cause to complain how little she knows of her greatest sons. Time may have hidden from the eye of biography the facts of Shakespeare's life, as time has revealed to the eye of criticism the grossness of his works and the purity of his rival's; but none need fear that the next age will have to lament the absence of materials for a life of Buchanan. Not once or twice has he told in simple prose of his sorrows and aspirations, his struggles and his aims. He has told us what good man gave him in his need a cup of cold water, and what bad man accused him of sycophancy in the expression of his thanks. He has told us what advantage was taken of his tender age by heartless publishers, what construction was put upon his gushing gratitude by heartless reviewers. He has told us that he never can forget his first friends; he has shown us that he never can forget himself. He has told us that the versicles of one David Gray, a poor young poeticule of the same breed as his panegyrist (who however, it should in fairness be said, died without giving any sign of future distinction in the field of pseudonymous libel), will be read when the works of other contemporaries "have gone to the limbo of affettuosos." (May I suggest that the library edition of Mr. Buchanan's collected works should be furnished with a glossary for the use of students unskilled in the varieties of the Buchananese dialect? Justly contemptuous as he has shown himself of all foreign affectations of speech or style in an English writer, such a remarkable word in its apparent defiance of analogy as the one last quoted is not a little perplexing to their ignorance. I hardly think it can be Scotch; at least to a southern eye it bears no recognizable affinity to the language of Burns.) In like manner, if we may trust the evidence of Byron, did Porson prophesy of Southey that his epics would be read when Homer and Virgil were forgotten; and in like manner may the humblest of his contemporaries prophesy that Mr. Buchanan's idyls will be read by generations which have forgotten the idyls of Theocritus and of Landor, of Tennyson and of Chénier.

In that singularly interesting essay on "his own tentatives" from which we have already taken occasion to glean certain flowers of comparative criticism Mr. Buchanan remarks of this contemporary that he seems rather fond of throwing stones in his (Mr. Buchanan's) direction. This contemporary, however,[47] is not in the habit of throwing stones; it is a pastime which he leaves to the smaller fry of the literary gutter. These it is sometimes not unamusing to watch as they dodge and shirk round the street-corner after the discharge of their popgun pellet, with the ready plea on their lips that it was not this boy but that—not the good boy Robert, for instance, but the rude boy Thomas. But there is probably only one man living who could imagine it worth his contemporary's while to launch the smallest stone from his sling in such a direction as that—who could conceive the very idlest of marksmen to be capable of taking aim unprovoked at[48] so pitiful a target. Mr. Buchanan and his nursing journals have informed us that to his other laurels he is entitled to add those of an accomplished sportsman. Surely he must know that there are animals which no one counts as game—which are classed under quite another head than that. Their proper designation it is needless here to repeat; it is one that suffices to exempt them from the honour and the danger common to creatures of a higher kind. Of their natural history I did not know enough till now to remark without surprise that specimens of the race may be found which are ambitious to be ranked among objects of sport. For my part, as long as I am not suspected of any inclination to join in the

chase, such an one should be welcome to lay that flattering unction
to his soul, and believe himself in secret one of the nobler beasts
of game:[49] even though it were but a weasel that would fain pass
muster as a hart of grice. It must no doubt be "very soothing" to
Mr. Buchanan's modesty to imagine himself the object of such
notice as he claims to have received; but we may observe from
how small a seed so large a growth of self-esteem may shoot up:—

σμικροῦ γένοιτ᾽ ἂν σπέρματος μέγας πυθμήν.

From[50] a slight passing mention of "idyls of the gutter and the
gibbet," in a passage referring to the idyllic schools of our day,
Mr. Buchanan has built up this fabric of induction; he is led by
even so much notice as this to infer that his work must be to the
writer an object of especial attention, and even (God save the
mark!) of especial attack. He is welcome to hug himself in that
fond belief, and fool himself to the top of his bent; but he will
hardly persuade any one else that to find his "neck-verse" merely
repulsive—[51] to feel no responsive vibration to "the intense loving
tenderness" of his street-walker[52] as she neighs and brays over her
"gallows-carrion"—[53] is the same thing as to deny the infinite value,
the incalculable significance, to a great poet, of such matters as this
luckless poeticule has here taken into[54] his "hangman's hands."
Neither the work nor the workman is to be judged by the casual
preferences of social convention. It is not more praiseworthy or
more pardonable to write bad verse about costermongers and
gaol-birds than to write bad verse about kings and knights; nor
(as would otherwise naturally be the case) is it to be expected that
because some among the greatest of poets have been born among
the poorest of men, therefore the literature of a nation is to suffer
joyfully an inundation or eruption of rubbish from all threshers,
cobblers, and milkwomen who now, as in the age of Pope, of
Johnson, or of Byron, may be stung to madness by the gadfly of
poetic ambition. As in one rank we find for a single Byron a score
of Roscommons, Mulgraves, and Winchilseas, so in another rank
we find for a single Burns a score of Ducks, Bloomfields, and
Yearsleys. And if it does not follow that a poet must be great
if he be but of low birth, neither does it follow that a poem must
be good if it be but written on a subject of low life. The sins and

sorrows of all that suffer wrong, the oppressions that are done under the sun, the dark days and shining deeds of the poor whom society casts out and crushes down, are assuredly material for poetry of a most high order; for the heroic passion of Victor Hugo's, for the angelic passion of Mrs. Browning's.[55] Let another such arise to do such work as "Les Pauvres Gens" or the "Cry of the Children," and there will be no lack of response to that singing. But they who can only "grate on their scrannel-pipes of wretched straw" some pitiful "idyl" to milk the maudlin eyes of the nursing journals[56] must be content with such applause as their own; for in higher latitudes they will find none.

It is not my purpose in this little scientific excursion to remark further than may be necessary on the symptoms of a poetical sort which the skilful eye may discern in the immediate objects of examination. To play the critic of their idyllic or satirical verse is not an office to which my ambition can aspire. Nevertheless, in the process of research, it may be useful to take note of the casual secretions observable in a fine live specimen of the breed in which we are interested, as well as of its general properties; for thus we may be the better able to determine, if we find that worth while, its special and differential attributes. I have therefore given a first and last glance to the poetic excretions of the present subject. Even from such things as these there might be something to learn, if men would bring to a task so unpromising and uninviting the patient eye and humble spirit of investigation by experiment. Such investigation would secure them against the common critical fallacy of assuming that a poem must be good because written on a subject, and it may be written with an aim, not unworthy of a better man than the writer; that a bad poem, for instance, on the life of our own day and the sorrows of our own people can only be condemned by those who would equally condemn a good poem on the same subject; who would admit[57] nothing as fit matter for artistic handling which[58] was not of a more remote and ideal kind than this: a theory invaluable to all worthless and ambitious journeymen of verse, who, were it once admitted as a law, would have only the trouble left them of selecting the subject whereon to emit their superfluity of metrical matter. Akin to this is a fallacy more amiable if not less absurd; the exact converse of the old superstition that anything written "by a person of quality" must be precious and praiseworthy. The same unreasoning and valueless admiration is now poured out at the feet of almost any one who comes forward under the contrary plea, as a poet of the people; and men forget that by this promiscuous effusion of praise they betray as complete a disbelief in any real equality of natural rank as did those who fell down before their idols of the other class. Such critics seem bent on verifying the worn old jest of the Irish reformer: "Is not one man as good as another; ay, and a deal better too?" No one now writes or speaks as if he supposed that every man born in what is called the aristocratic class must needs and naturally, if he should make verses, take his place beside Shelley or Byron; the assumption would be felt on all hands as an impertinence rather than a compliment offered to that class; and how can it be other than an impertinence offered to a larger class to assume, or pretend to assume, that any one born in the opposite rank who may be put forward as a poet must naturally be the equal of Béranger or of Burns? Such an assumption is simply an inverted form of tuft-hunting; it implies at once the arrogant condescension of the patron to his parasite, and the lurking contempt of the parasite for his patron:[59] not a beautiful or profitable combination of qualities.

A critic in the *Contemporary Review,* but neither Robert Maitland nor Thomas Buchanan, once took occasion to inquire with emphatic sarcasm, what did Shelley care, or what does another writer whom he did the honour to call the second Shelley—how undeservedly no one can be more conscious than the person so unduly exalted—care for the people, for the sufferings and the cause of the poor? To be accused of caring no more for the people than Shelley did may seem to some men much the same thing as to be accused of caring no more for France than Victor Hugo does, or for Italy than did one whose name I will not now bring into such a paper as this. But to some men, on the other hand, it may appear that this cruel charge will serve to explain the jealous acrimony with which the writer thus condemned and dismissed in such evil company "seems" incessantly and secretly to have assailed the fame of Mr. Buchanan—the rancorous malignity with which he must have long looked up from the hiding-place of a furtive obscurity towards the unapproachable heights, the unattainable honours, of the mountains climbed and the prizes grasped by the Poet of the Poor. It mattered little that his disguise was impenetrable to every other eye; that those nearest him had no suspicion of the villainous design which must ever have been at work in his brain, even when itself unconscious of itself; that his left hand knew not what his right hand was doing (as it most certainly did not) when it cast stones at the sweet lyrist of the slums; masked and cloaked, under the thickest muffler of anonymous or pseudonymous counterfeit, the stealthy and cowering felon stood revealed to the naked eye of honesty—stood detected, convicted, exposed to the frank and fearless gaze of Mr. Buchanan. Can a figure more pitiful or more shameful be conceived? The only atonement that can ever be made for such a rascally form of malevolence is that which is here offered in the way of confession and penance; the only excuse that can be advanced for such a viperous method of attack is that envy and hatred of his betters have ever been the natural signs and the inevitable appanages of a bad poet, whether he had studied in the fleshly or the skinny school. Remembering this, we can but too easily understand how Mr. Buchanan may have excited the general ill-will of his inferiors; we may deplore, but we cannot wonder, that the author of "Liz" and "Nell" should have aroused a sense of impotent envy in the author of "Jenny" and "Sister Helen"; it would not surprise though it could not but grieve us to hear that the author of "The Earthly Paradise" was inwardly consumed by the canker of jealousy when he thought of the "Legends of Inverburn"; while with burning cheeks and downcast eyes it must be confessed that the author of "Atalanta in Calydon" may well be the prey of rancour yet more keen than theirs when he looks on the laurels that naturally prevent him from sleeping—the classic chaplets that crown the author of "Undertones."[60]

It is but too well known that the three minor minstrels above named, who may perhaps be taken as collectively equivalent in station and intelligence to the single Buchanan, have long been banded together in a dark and unscrupulous league to decry all works and all reputations but their own. In the first and third persons of this unholy trinity the reptile passions of selfishness and envy have constantly broken out in every variety of ugliness; in the leprous eruption of naked insult, in the cancerous process of that rank and rotten malevolence which works its infectious way by hints and indications, in the nervous spasm of epileptic agony which convulses the whole frame of the soul at another's praise, and ends in a sort of moral tetanus at sight of another's triumph. That thus, and thus only, have their wretched spirits been affected by the spectacle of good and great things done by other men, the whole course of their artistic life and the whole tenor of their critical or illustrative work may be cited against them to bear witness. The least reference to the latter will suffice to show the narrow range and the insincere assumption of their hollow and self-centered sympathies, the poisonous bitterness and the rancorous meanness of their furtive and virulent antipathies. Thomas Maitland, in his character of the loyal detective, has also done the state of letters some service by exposing the shameless reciprocity of systematic applause kept up on all hands by this "mutual admiration society." Especial attention should be given to the candid and clear-sighted remarks of the critic on the "puffing" reviews of his accomplices by the senior member of the gang, and of the third party to this plot by both his colleagues in corruption and conspiracy. If any one outside their obscure and restricted circle of reciprocal intrigue and malignant secrecy has ever won from any of them the slightest dole of reluctant and grudging commendation, it has been easily traceable to the muddy source of self-interest or of sycophancy. To men of such long-established eminence and influence that it must evidently bring more of immediate profit to applaud them than to revile, there are writers who will ever be at hand to pour the nauseous libations of a parasite. Envy itself in such natures will change places on alternate days with self-interest; and a hand which the poor cur's tooth would otherwise be fain to bite, his tongue will then be fain to beslaver. More especially when there is a chance of discharging its natural venom in the very act of that servile caress; when the obsequious lip finds a way to insinuate by flattery of one superior some stealthy calumny of another. "Ah, my lord and master," says the jackal to the lion (or for that matter to any other animal from whose charity or contempt it may hope for toleration and a stray bone or so now and then), "observe how all other living creatures belong but to some sub-leonine class,* some school of dependents and subordinates such as the poor slave who has now the honour to lick your foot!" This is a somewhat ignoble attitude on the poor slave's part, though excusable perhaps in a hungry four-footed brute; but if any such biped as a minor poet were to play such a game as this of the jackal's, what word could we properly apply to him? and what inference should we be justified in drawing as to the origin of his vicious antipathy to other names not less eminent than his chosen patron's? Might we not imagine that some of the men at whose heels he now snaps instead of cringing have found it necessary before now to "spurn him like a cur out of their way"? It is of course possible that a man may honestly admire Mr. Tennyson who feels nothing but scorn and distaste for Mr. Carlyle or Mr. Thackeray; but if the latter feeling, expressed as it may be with barefaced and open-mouthed insolence, be as genuine and natural to him as the former, sprung from no petty grudge or privy spite, but reared in the normal soil or manured with the native compost of his mind,—the admiration of such an one is hardly a thing to be desired.

If however any one of that envious and currish triumvirate whom the open voice of honest criticism has already stigmatized should think in future of setting a trap for the illustrious object of their common malice, he will, it is to be hoped, take heed that his feet be not caught in his own snare. He will remember that the judgment of men now or hereafter on the work of an artist in any kind does not wholly depend on the evidence or the opinions of any Jack Alias or Tom Alibi who may sneak into court and out again when detected. He will not think to protect himself from the degradation of public exposure by the assumption of some such pseudonym as Joseph Surface or Seth Pecksniff. He will not feel that all is safe when he has assured the public that a review article alternating between covert praise of himself and

---

* If we could imagine about 1820 some parasitic poeticule of the order of Kirke White classifying together Coleridge and Keats, Byron and Shelley, as members of "the sub-Wordsworthian school," we might hope to find an intellectual ancestor for Mr. Robert Buchanan; but that hope is denied us:[61] we are reduced to believe that Mr. Buchanan must be autochthonous, or sprung perhaps from a cairngorm pebble cast behind him by the hand of some Scotch Deucalion.

overt abuse of his superiors was only through the merest "inad-vertence"[62] not issued in his own name; that it never would have appeared under the signature of Mr. Alias but that Mr. Alibi hap-pened by the most untoward of accidents to be just then away "in his yacht" on a cruise among "the western Hebrides"; otherwise, and but for the blundering oversight of some unhappy publisher or editor, the passages which refer with more or less stealthy and suggestive insinuation of preference or of praise to the avowed publications of Mr. Alibi would have come before us with the warrant of that gentleman's honoured name. Credat Judæus Apella! but even the foolishest of our furtive triumvirate will hardly, I should imagine, expect that any son of circumcision or of uncircumcision would believe such a "legend" or give ear to such an "idyl" as that. Rather will he be inclined to meditate some-what thus, after the fashion of the American poetess at Elijah Pogram's levee: "To be presented to a Maitland," he will reflect, "by a Buchanan, indeed, an impressive moment is it on what we call our feelings. But why we call them so, or why impressed they are, or if impressed they are at all, or if at all we are, or if there really is, oh gasping one! a Maitland or a Buchanan, or any active principle to which we give those titles, is a topic spirit-searching, light-abandoned, much too vast to enter on at this unlooked-for crisis." Or it may be he will call to mind an old couplet of some such fashion as this:—

> A man of letters would Crispinus be;
> He is a man of letters; yes, of three.

How many names he may have on hand it might not be so easy to resolve: nor which of these, if any, may be genuine; but for the three letters he need look no further than his Latin dictionary; if such a reference be not something more than superfluous for a writer of "epiludes" who renders "domus exilis Plutonia" by "a Plutonian house of exiles": a version not properly to be criticized in any "school" by simple application of goose-quill to paper.*

* I am reminded here of another "contemporary"[63] somewhat more notorious than this classic namesake and successor of George Buchanan, but like him a man of many and questionable names, who lately had occasion, while figuring on a more public stage than that of literature, to translate the words "Laus Deo semper" by "The laws of God for ever." It must evidently be from the same source that Mr.

The disciple on whom "the deep delicious stream of the Latinity" of Petronius has made such an impression that he finds also a deep delicious morality in the pure and sincere pages of a book from which less pure-minded readers and writers less sincere than himself are compelled to turn away sick and silent with disgust after a second vain attempt to look it over—this loving student and satellite so ready to shift a trencher at the banquet of Trimalchio— has less of tolerance, we are scarcely surprised to find, for Æschylean Greece than for Neronian Rome. Among the imperfect and obsolete productions of the Greek stage he does indeed assign a marked pre-eminence over all others to the Persæ. To the famous epitaph of Æschylus which tells only in four terse lines of his service as a soldier against the Persians, there should now be added a couplet in commemoration of the precedence granted to his play by a poet who would not stoop to imitate and a student who need not hesitate to pass sentence. Against this good opinion, however, we are bound to set on record the memorable expression of that deep and thoughtful contempt which a mind so enlightened and a soul so exalted must naturally feel for "the shallow and barbarous myth of Prometheus." Well may this incomparable critic, this unique and sovereign arbiter of thought and letters ancient and modern, remark with compassion and condemnation how inevitably a training in Grecian literature must tend to "emas-

---

Buchanan and the Tichborne claimant have drawn their first and last draught of "the humanities." Fellow-students, whether at Stonyhurst or elsewhere, they ought certainly to have been. Can it be the rankling recollection of some boyish quarrel in which he came by the worst of it that keeps alive in the noble soul of Mr. Buchanan a dislike of "fleshly persons?" The result would be worthy of such a "fons et origo mali"—a phrase, I may add for the benefit of such scholars, which is not adequately or exactly rendered by "the fount of original sin." Perhaps some day we may be gratified—but let us hope without any necessary intervention of lawyers—by some further discovery of the early associations which may have clustered around the promising boyhood of Thomas Maitland. Meantime it is a comfort to reflect that the assumption of a forged name for a dirty purpose does not always involve the theft of thousands, or the ruin of any reputation more valuable than that of a literary underling. May we not now also hope that Mr. Buchanan's fellow-scholar will be the next (in old-world phrase) to "oblige the reading public" with his views on ancient and modern literature? For such a work, whether undertaken in the calm of Newgate or the seclusion of the Hebrides, or any other haunt of lettered ease and leisure, he surely could not fail to find a publisher who in his turn would not fail to find him an *alibi* whenever necessary—whether eastward or westward of St. Kilda.

culate" the student so trained: and well may we congratulate ourselves that no such process as robbed of all strength and manhood the intelligence of Milton has had power to impair the
virility of Mr. Buchanan's robust and masculine genius. To that
strong and severe figure we turn from the sexless and nerveless
company of shrill-voiced singers who share with Milton the curse
of enforced effeminacy; from the pitiful soprano notes of such
dubious creatures as Marlowe, Jonson, Chapman, Gray, Coleridge,
Shelley, Landor, "cum semiviro comitatu," we avert our ears to
catch the higher and manlier harmonies of a poet with all his
natural parts and powers complete. For truly, if love or knowledge
of ancient art and wisdom be the sure mark of "emasculation,"
and the absence of any taint of such love or any tincture of such
knowledge (as then in consistency it must be) the supreme sign
of perfect manhood, Mr. Robert Buchanan should be amply competent to renew the thirteenth labour of Hercules.

> One would not be a young maid in his way
> For more than blushing comes to.

Nevertheless, in a country where (as Mr. Carlyle says in his essay
on Diderot) indecent exposure is an offence cognizable at police-
offices, it might have been as well for him to uncover with less
immodest publicity the gigantic nakedness of his ignorance. Any
sense of shame must probably be as alien to the Heracleidan blood
as any sense of fear; but the spectators of such an exhibition may
be excused if they could wish that at least the shirt of Nessus
or another were happily at hand to fling over the more than human display of that massive and muscular impudence, in all the
abnormal development of its monstrous proportions. It is possible
that our Scottish demigod of song has made too long a sojourn in
"the land of Lorne," and learnt from his Highland comrades to
dispense in public with what is not usually discarded in any
British latitude far south of "the western Hebrides."

At this point, and even after this incomparable windfall in the
way of entomology, I begin to doubt whether after all I shall ever
make any way as a scientific student. The savours, the forms, the
sounds, the contortions, of the singular living things which this
science commands us to submit to examination, need a stouter

stomach to cope with them than mine. No doubt they have their reasons for being; they were probably meant for some momentary action and passion of their own, harmful or harmless; and how can the naturalist suppose that merely by accurate analysis of their phenomena he has gauged the secret of their mysterious existence? It is so hard to see the reason why they should be, that we are compelled to think the reason must be very grave.

And if once we cease to regard such things scientifically, there is assuredly no reason why we should regard them at all. Historically considered, they have no interest whatever; the historian discerns no perceptible variation in their tribe for centuries on centuries. It is only because this age is not unlike other ages that the children of Zoilus whet their teeth against your epic, the children of Rymer against your play; the children—no, not the children; let us at least be accurate—the successors of Fréron and Desfontaines lift up their throats against your worship of women:

Monsieur Veuillot t'appelle avec esprit citrouille;

Mr. Buchanan indicates to all Hebridean eyes the flaws and affectations in your style, as in that of an amatory foreigner; Mr. Lowell assures his market that the best coin you have to offer is brass, and more than hints that it is stolen brass—whether from his own or another forehead, he scorns to specify; and the Montrouge Jesuit, the Grubstreet[64] poet, the Mayflower Puritan, finds each his perfect echo in his natural child; in the first voice you catch the twang of Garasse and Nonotte, in the second of Flecknoe and Dennis, in the third of Tribulation Wholesome and Zeal-of-the-Land Busy. Perhaps then after all their use is to show that the age is not a bastard, but the legitimate heir and representative of other centuries; degenerate, if so it please you to say—all ages have been degenerate in their turn—as to its poets and workers, but surely not degenerate as to these. Poor then as it may be in other things, the very lapse of years which has left it weak may help it more surely to determine than stronger ages could the nature of the critical animal. Has not popular opinion passed through wellnigh the same stages with regard to the critic and to the toad? What was thought in the time of Shakespeare by dukes as well as peasants, we may all find written in his verse; but we know now on taking up a Buchanan that, though very ugly, it is not in the least venomous, and assuredly wears no precious jewel in its head. Yet is it rather like a newt or blindworm than a toad; there is a mendacious air of the old serpent about it at first sight; and the thing is not even viperous: its sting is as false as its tongue is; its very venom is a lie. But when once we have seen the fang, though innocuous, protrude from a mouth which would fain distil poison and can only distil froth, we need no revelation to assure us that the doom of the creature is to go upon its belly and eat dust all the days of its life.

DEDICATORY
EPISTLE

To my best and dearest friend I dedicate the first collected edition of my poems, and to him I address what I have to say on the occasion.

You will agree with me that it is impossible for any man to undertake the task of commentary, however brief and succinct, on anything he has done or tried to do, without incurring the charge of egoism. But there are two kinds of egoism, the furtive and the frank: and the outspoken and open-hearted candour of Milton and Wordsworth, Corneille and Hugo, is not the least or the lightest of their claims to the regard as well as the respect or the reverence of their readers. Even if I were worthy to claim kinship with the lowest or with the highest of these deathless names, I would not seek to shelter myself under the shadow of its authority. The question would still remain open on all sides. Whether it is worth while for any man to offer any remarks or for any other man to read his remarks on his own work, his own ambition, or his own attempts, he cannot of course determine. If there are great examples of abstinence from such a doubtful enterprise, there are likewise great examples to the contrary. As long as the writer can succeed in evading the kindred charges and the cognate risks of vanity and humility, there can be no reason why he should not undertake it. And when he has nothing to regret and nothing to recant, when he finds nothing that he could wish to cancel, to alter, or to unsay, in any page he has ever laid before his reader, he need not be seriously troubled by the inevitable consciousness that the work of his early youth is not and cannot be unnaturally unlike the work of a very young man. This would be no excuse for it, if it were in any sense bad work: if it be so, no apology would avail; and I certainly have none to offer.

It is now thirty-six years since my first volume of miscellaneous verse, lyrical and dramatic and elegiac and generally heterogeneous, had as quaint a reception and as singular a fortune as I have

ever heard or read of. I do not think you will differ from my
opinion that what is best in it cannot be divided from what is not
so good by any other line of division than that which marks off
mature from immature execution—in other words, complete from
incomplete conception. For its author the most amusing and satisfying result of the clatter aroused by it was the deep diversion
of collating and comparing the variously inaccurate verdicts of
the scornful or mournful censors who insisted on regarding all
the studies of passion or sensation attempted or achieved in it as
either confessions of positive fact or excursions of absolute fancy.
There are photographs from life in the book; and there are
sketches from imagination. Some which keen-sighted criticism has
dismissed with a smile as ideal or imaginary were as real and actual
as they well could be: others which have been taken for obvious
transcripts from memory were utterly fantastic or dramatic. If
the two kinds cannot be distinguished, it is surely rather a credit
than a discredit to an artist whose medium or material has more
in common with a musician's than with a sculptor's. Friendly and
kindly critics, English and foreign, have detected ignorance of the
subject in poems taken straight from the life, and have protested
that they could not believe me were I to swear that poems entirely
or mainly fanciful were not faithful expressions or transcriptions
of the writer's actual experience and personal emotion. But I need
not remind you that all I have to say about this book was said
once for all in the year of its publication: I have nothing to add to
my notes then taken, and I have nothing to retract from them. To
parade or to disclaim experience of passion or of sorrow, of
pleasure or of pain, is the habit and the sign of a school which
has never found a disciple among the better sort of English poets,
and which I know to be no less pitifully contemptible in your
opinion than in mine.

In my next work it should be superfluous to say that there is
no touch of dramatic impersonation or imaginary emotion. The
writer of "Songs before Sunrise," from the first line to the last,
wrote simply in submissive obedience to Sir Philip Sidney's precept—"Look in thine heart, and write." The dedication of these
poems, and the fact that the dedication was accepted, must be
sufficient evidence of this. They do not pretend and they were

never intended to be merely the metrical echoes, or translations into lyric verse, of another man's doctrine. Mazzini was no more a Pope or a Dictator than I was a parasite or a papist. Dictation and inspiration are rather different things. These poems, and others which followed or preceded them in print, were inspired by such faith as is born of devotion and reverence: not by such faith, if faith it may be called, as is synonymous with servility or compatible with prostration of an abject or wavering spirit and a submissive or dethroned intelligence. You know that I never pretended to see eye to eye with my illustrious friends and masters, Victor Hugo and Giuseppe Mazzini, in regard to the positive and passionate confidence of their sublime and purified theology. Our betters ought to know better than we: they would be the last to wish that we should pretend to their knowledge, or assume a certitude which is theirs and is not ours. But on one point we surely cannot but be at one with them: that the spirit and the letter of all other than savage and barbarous religions are irreconcilably at variance, and that prayer or homage addressed to an image of our own or of other men's making, be that image avowedly material or conventionally spiritual, is the affirmation of idolatry with all its attendant atrocities, and the negation of all belief, all reverence, and all love, due to the noblest object of human worship that humanity can realise or conceive. Thus much the exercise of our common reason might naturally suffice to show us: but when its evidence is confirmed and fortified by the irrefragable and invariable evidence of history, there is no room for further dispute or fuller argument on a subject now visibly beyond reach and eternally beyond need of debate or demonstration. I know not whether it may or may not be worth while to add that every passing word I have since thought fit to utter on any national or political question has been as wholly consistent with the principles which I then did my best to proclaim and defend as any apostasy from the faith of all republicans in the fundamental and final principle of union, voluntary if possible and compulsory if not, would have been ludicrous in the impudence of its inconsistency with those simple and irreversible principles. Monarchists and anarchists may be advocates of national dissolution and reactionary division: republicans cannot be. The first and last article of their creed is unity:

the most grinding and crushing tyranny of a convention, a directory, or a despot, is less incompatible with republican faith than the fissiparous democracy of disunionists or communalists.

If the fortunes of my lyrical work were amusingly eccentric and accidental, the varieties of opinion which have saluted the appearance of my plays have been, or have seemed to my humility, even more diverting and curious. I have been told by reviewers of note and position that a single one of them is worth all my lyric and otherwise undramatic achievements or attempts: and I have been told on equal or similar authority that, whatever I may be in any other field, as a dramatist I am demonstrably nothing. My first if not my strongest ambition was to do something worth doing, and not utterly unworthy of a young countryman of Marlowe the teacher and Webster the pupil of Shakespeare, in the line of work which those three poets had left as a possibly unattainable example for ambitious Englishmen. And my first book, written while yet under academic or tutorial authority, bore evidence of that ambition in every line. I should be the last to deny that it also bore evidence of the fact that its writer had no more notion of dramatic or theatrical construction than the authors of "Tamburlaine the Great," "King Henry VI.," and "Sir Thomas Wyatt." Not much more, you may possibly say, was discernible in "Chastelard": a play also conceived and partly written by a youngster not yet emancipated from servitude to college rule. I fear that in the former volume there had been little if any promise of power to grapple with the realities and subtleties of character and of motive: that whatever may be in it of promise or of merit must be sought in the language and the style of such better passages as may perhaps be found in single and separable speeches of Catherine and of Rosamond. But in "Chastelard" there are two figures and a sketch in which I certainly seem to see something of real and evident life. The sketch of Darnley was afterwards filled out and finished in the subsequent tragedy of "Bothwell." That ambitious, conscientious, and comprehensive piece of work is of course less properly definable as a tragedy than by the old Shakespearean term of a chronicle history. The radical difference between tragic history and tragedy of either the classic or the romantic order, and consequently between the laws which govern the one and the principles which guide the other, you have yourself made clear and familiar to all capable students. This play of mine was not, I think, inaccurately defined as an epic drama in the French verses of dedication which were acknowledged by the greatest of all French poets in a letter from which I dare only quote one line of Olympian judgment and god-like generosity. "Occuper ces deux cimes, cela n'est donné qu'à vous." Nor will I refrain from the confession that I cannot think it an epic or a play in which any one part is sacrificed to any other, any subordinate figure mishandled or neglected or distorted or effaced for the sake of the predominant and central person. And, though this has nothing or less than nothing to do with any question of poetic merit or demerit, of dramatic success or un-success, I will add that I took as much care and pains as though I had been writing or compiling a history of the period to do loyal justice to all the historic figures which came within the scope of my dramatic or poetic design. There is not one which I have designedly altered or intentionally modified: it is of course for others to decide whether there is one which is not the living like-ness of an actual or imaginable man.

The third part of this trilogy, as far as I know or remember, found favour only with the only man in England who could speak on the subject of historic drama with the authority of an expert and a master. The generally ungracious reception of "Mary Stuart" gave me neither surprise nor disappointment: the cordial approbation or rather the generous applause of Sir Henry Taylor gave me all and more than all the satisfaction I could ever have looked for in recompense of as much painstaking and conscien-tious though interesting and enjoyable work as can ever, I should imagine, have been devoted to the completion of any comparable design. Private and personal appreciation I have always thought and often found more valuable and delightful than all possible or imaginable clamour of public praise. This preference will perhaps be supposed to influence my opinion if I avow that I think I have never written anything worthier of such reward than the closing tragedy which may or may not have deserved but which certainly received it.

My first attempt to do something original in English which might in some degree reproduce for English readers the likeness of a Greek tragedy, with possibly something more of its true poetic life and charm than could have been expected from the authors of "Caractacus" and "Merope," was perhaps too exuberant and effusive in its dialogue, as it certainly was too irregular in the occasional license of its choral verse, to accomplish the design or achieve the success which its author should have aimed at. It may or may not be too long as a poem: it is, I fear, too long for a poem of the kind to which it belongs or aims at belonging. Poetical and mathematical truth are so different that I doubt, however unwilling I may naturally be to doubt, whether it can truthfully be said of "Atalanta in Calydon" that the whole is greater than any part of it. I hope it may be, and I can honestly say no more. Of "Erechtheus" I venture to believe with somewhat more confidence that it can. Either poem, by the natural necessity of its kind and structure, has its crowning passage or passages which cannot, however much they may lose by detachment from their context, lose as much as the crowning scene or scenes of an English or Shakespearean play, as opposed to an Æschylean or Sophoclean tragedy, must lose and ought to lose by a similar separation. The two best things in these two Greek plays, the antiphonal lamentation for the dying Meleager and the choral presentation of stormy battle between the forces of land and sea, lose less by such division from the main body of the poem than would those scenes in "Bothwell" which deal with the turning-point in the life of Mary Stuart on the central and conclusive day of Carberry Hill.

It might be thought pedantic or pretentious in a modern poet to divide his poems after the old Roman fashion into sections and classes: I must confess that I should like to see this method applied, were it but by way of experiment in a single edition, to the work of the leading poets of our own country and century: to see, for instance, their lyrical and elegiac works ranged and registered apart, each kind in a class of its own, such as is usually reserved, I know not why, for sonnets only. The apparent formality of such an arrangement as would give us, for instance, the odes of Coleridge and Shelley collected into a distinct reservation or division might possibly be more than compensated to the more capable among students by the gain in ethical or spiritual symmetry and æsthetic or intellectual harmony. The ode or hymn—I need remind no probable reader that the terms are synonymous in the speech of Pindar—asserts its primacy or pre-eminence over other forms of poetry in the very name which defines or proclaims it as essentially the song; as something above all less pure and absolute kinds of song by the very nature and law of its being. The Greek form, with its regular arrangement of turn, return, and after-song, is not to be imitated because it is Greek, but to be adopted because it is best: the very best, as a rule, that could be imagined for lyrical expression of the thing conceived or lyrical aspiration towards the aim imagined. The rhythmic reason of its rigid but not arbitrary law lies simply and solely in the charm of its regular variations. This can be given in English as clearly and fully, if not so sweetly and subtly, as in Greek; and should, therefore, be expected and required in an English poem of the same nature and proportion. The Sapphic or Alcaic Ode, a simple sequence of identical stanzas, could be imitated or revived in Latin by translators or disciples: the scheme of it is exquisitively adequate and sufficient for comparatively short flights of passion or emotion, ardent or contemplative and personal or patriotic; but what can be done in English could not be attempted in Latin. It seems strange to me, our language being what it is, that our literature should be no richer than it is in examples of the higher or at least the more capacious and ambitious kind of ode. Not that the full Pindaric form of threefold or triune structure need be or should be always adopted: but without an accurately corresponsive or antiphonal scheme of music even the master of masters, who is Coleridge, could not produce, even through the superb and enchanting melodies of such a poem as his "Dejection," a fit and complete companion, a full and perfect rival, to such a poem as his ode on France.

The title of ode may more properly and fairly be so extended as to cover all lyrical poems in stanzas or couplets than so strained as to include a lawless lyric of such irregular and uneven build as Coleridge only and hardly could make acceptable or admissible among more natural and lawful forms of poetry. Law, not lawlessness, is the natural condition of poetic life; but the law must itself be poetic and not pedantic, natural and not conventional. It would be a trivial precision or restriction which would refuse the title of ode to the stanzas of Milton or the heptameters of Aristophanes; that glorious form of lyric verse which a critic of our own day, as you may not impossibly remember, has likened with such magnificent felicity of comparison to the gallop of the horses of the sun. Nor, I presume, should this title be denied to a poem written in the more modest metre—more modest as being shorter by a foot—which was chosen for those twin poems of antiphonal correspondence in subject and in sound, the "Hymn to Proserpine" and the "Hymn of Man": the deathsong of spiritual decadence and the birthsong of spiritual renascence. Perhaps, too, my first stanzas addressed to Victor Hugo may be ranked as no less of an ode than that on the insurrection in Candia: a poem which attracted, whether or not it may have deserved, the notice and commendation of Mazzini: from whom I received, on the occasion of its appearance, a letter which was the beginning of my personal intercourse with the man whom I had always revered above all other men on earth. But for this happy accident I might not feel disposed to set much store by my first attempt at a regular ode of orthodox or legitimate construction; I doubt whether it quite succeeded in evading the criminal risk and the capital offence of formality; at least until the change of note in the closing epode gave fuller scope and freer play of wing to the musical expression. But in my later ode on Athens, absolutely faithful as it is in form to the strictest type and the most stringent law of Pindaric hymnology, I venture to believe that there is no more sign of this infirmity than in the less classically regulated poem on the Armada; which, though built on a new scheme, is nevertheless in its way, I think, a legitimate ode, by right of its regularity in general arrangement of corresponsive divisions. By the test of these two poems I am content that my claims should be decided and my station determined as a lyric poet in the higher sense of the term; a craftsman in the most ambitious line of his art that ever aroused or ever can arouse the emulous aspiration of his kind.

Even had I ever felt the same impulse to attempt and the same ambition to achieve the enterprise of epic or narrative that I had always felt with regard to lyric or dramatic work, I could never have proposed to myself the lowly and unambitious aim of competition with the work of so notable a contemporary workman in the humbler branch of that line as William Morris. No conception could have been further from my mind when I undertook to rehandle the deathless legend of Tristram than that of so modest and preposterous a trial of rivalry. My aim was simply to present that story, not diluted and debased as it had been in our own time by other hands, but undefaced by improvement and undeformed by transformation, as it was known to the age of Dante wherever the chronicles of romance found hearing, from Ercildoune to Florence: and not in the epic or romantic form of sustained or continuous narrative, but mainly through a succession of dramatic scenes or pictures with descriptive settings or backgrounds: the scenes being of the simplest construction, duologue or monologue, without so much as the classically permissible intervention of a third or fourth person. It is only in our native northern form of narrative poetry, on the old and unrivalled model of the English ballad, that I can claim to have done any work of the kind worth reference: unless the story of Balen should be considered as something other than a series or sequence of ballads. A more plausible objection was brought to bear against "Tristram of Lyonesse" than that of failure in an enterprise which I never thought of undertaking: the objection of an irreconcilable incongruity between the incidents of the old legend and the meditations on man and nature, life and death, chance and destiny, assigned to a typical hero of chivalrous romance. And this objection might be unanswerable if the slightest attempt had been made to treat the legend as in any possible sense historical or capable of either rational or ideal association with history, such as would assimilate the name and fame of Arthur to the name and fame of any actual and indisputable Alfred or Albert of the future. But the age when these romances actually lived and flourished side by side with the reviving legends of Thebes and Troy, not in the crude and bloodless forms of Celtic and archaic fancy but in the ampler and manlier developments of Teutonic and mediæval imagination, was the age of Dante and of Chaucer: an age in which men were only too prone to waste their time on the twin sciences of astrology and theology, to expend their energies in the jungle of pseudosophy or the morass of metaphysics. There is surely nothing more incongruous or anachronic in the soliloquy of Tristram after his separation from Iseult than in the lecture of Theseus after the obsequies of Arcite. Both heroes belong to the same impossible age of an imaginary world: and each has an equal right, should it so please his chronicler, to reason in the pauses of action and philosophise in the intervals of adventure. After all, the active men of the actual age of chivalry were not all of them mere muscular machines for martial or pacific exercise of their physical functions or abilities.

You would agree, if the point were worth discussion, that it might savour somewhat of pretension, if not of affectation, to be over particular in arrangement of poems according to subject rather than form, spirit rather than method, or motive rather than execution: and yet there might be some excuse for the fancy or the pedantry of such a classification as should set apart, for example, poems inspired by the influence of places, whether seen but once or familiar for years or associated with the earliest memories within cognisance or record of the mind, and poems inspired by the emotions of regard or regret for the living or the dead; above all, by the rare and profound passion of reverence and love and faith which labours and rejoices to find utterance in some tributary sacrifice of song. Mere descriptive poetry of the prepense and formal kind is exceptionally if not proverbially liable to incur and to deserve the charge of dullness: it is unnecessary to emphasise or obtrude the personal note, the presence or the emotion of a spectator, but it is necessary to make it felt and keep it perceptible if the poem is to have life in it or even a right to live: felt as in Wordsworth's work it is always, perceptible as it is always in Shelley's. This note is more plain and positive than usual in the poem which attempts—at once a simple and an ambitious attempt—to render the contrast and the concord of night and day on Loch Torridon: it is, I think, duly sensible though implicitly subdued in four poems of the West Undercliff, born or begotten of sunset in the bay and moonlight on the cliffs, noon or morning in a living and shining garden, afternoon or twilight on one left flowerless and forsaken. Not to you or any other poet, nor indeed to the very humblest and simplest lover of poetry, will it seem incongruous or strange, suggestive of imperfect sympathy with life or deficient inspiration from nature, that the very words of Sappho should be heard and recognised in the notes of the nightingales, the glory of the presence of dead poets imagined in the presence of the glory of the sky, the lustre of their advent and their passage felt visible as in vision on the live and limpid floorwork of the cloudless and sunset-coloured sea. The half-brained creature to whom books are other than living things may see with the eyes of a bat and draw with the fingers of a mole his dullard's distinction between books and life: those who live the fuller life of a higher animal than he know that books are to poets as much part of that life as pictures are to painters or as music is to musicians, dead matter though they may be to the spiritually still-born children of dirt and dullness who find it possible and natural to live while dead in heart and brain. Marlowe and Shakespeare, Æschylus and Sappho, do not for us live only on the dusty shelves of libraries.

It is hardly probable that especial and familiar love of places should give any special value to verses written under the influence of their charm: no intimacy of years and no association with the past gave any colour of emotion to many other studies of English land and sea which certainly are no less faithful and possibly have no less spiritual or poetic life in them than the four to which I have just referred, whose localities lie all within the boundary of a mile or so. No contrast could be stronger than that between the majestic and exquisite glory of cliff and crag, lawn and woodland, garden and lea, to which I have done homage though assuredly I have not done justice in these four poems—"In the Bay," "On the Cliffs," "A Forsaken Garden," the dedication of "The Sisters" —and the dreary beauty, inhuman if not unearthly in its desolation, of the innumerable creeks and inlets, lined and paven with sea-flowers, which make of the salt marshes a fit and funereal setting, a fatal and appropriate foreground, for the supreme desolation of the relics of Dunwich; the beautiful and awful solitude of a wilderness on which the sea has forbidden man to build or live, overtopped and bounded by the tragic and ghastly solitude of a headland on which the sea has forbidden the works of human charity and piety to survive: between the dense and sand-encumbered tides which are eating the desecrated wreck and ruin of them all away, and the matchless magic, the ineffable fascination of the sea whose beauties and delights, whose translucent depths of water and divers-coloured banks of submarine foliage and flowerage, but faintly reflected in the stanzas of the little ode "Off Shore," complete the charm of the scenes as faintly sketched or shadowed forth in the poems just named, or the sterner and stranger magic of the seaboard to which tribute was paid in "An Autumn Vision," "A Swimmer's Dream," "On the South Coast," "Neap-tide": or, again, between the sterile stretches and sad limitless outlook of the shore which faces a hitherto undetermined and interminable sea, and the joyful and fateful beauty of the seas off Bamborough and the seas about Sark and Guernsey. But if there is enough of the human or personal note to bring into touch the various poems which deal with these various impressions, there may perhaps be no less of it discernible in such as try to render the effect of inland or woodland solitude—the splendid oppression of nature at noon which found utterance of old in words of such singular and everlasting significance as panic and nympholepsy.

The retrospect across many years over the many eulogistic and elegiac poems which I have inscribed or devoted to the commemoration or the panegyric of the living or the dead has this in it of pride and pleasure, that I find little to recant and nothing to repent on reconsideration of them all. If ever a word of tributary thanksgiving for the delight and the benefit of loyal admiration evoked in the spirit of a boy or aroused in the intelligence of a man may seem to exceed the limit of demonstrable accuracy, I have no apology to offer for any such aberration from the safe path of tepid praise or conventional applause. I can truly say with Shelley that I have been fortunate in friendships: I might add if I cared, as he if he had cared might have added, that I have been no less fortunate in my enemies than in my friends; and this, though by comparison a matter of ineffable insignificance, can hardly be to any rational and right-minded man a matter of positive indifference. Rather should it be always a subject for thankfulness and self-congratulation if a man can honestly and reasonably feel assured that his friends and foes alike have been always and at almost all points the very men he would have chosen, had choice and foresight been allowed him, at the very outset of his career in life. I should never, when a boy, have dared to dream that as a man I might possibly be admitted to the personal acquaintance of the three living gods, I do not say of my idolatry, for idolatry is a term inapplicable where the gods are real and true, but of my whole-souled and single-hearted worship: and yet, when writing of Landor, of Mazzini, and of Hugo, I write of men who have honoured me with the assurance and the evidence of their cordial and affectionate regard. However inadequate and unworthy may be my tribute to their glory when living and their memory when dead, it is that of one whose gratitude and devotion found unforgettable favour in their sight. And I must be allowed to add that the redeeming quality of entire and absolute sincerity may be claimed on behalf of every line I have written in honour of friends, acquaintances, or strangers. My tribute to Richard Burton was not more genuine in its expression than my tribute to Christina Rossetti. Two noble human creatures more utterly unlike each other it would be unspeakably impossible to conceive; but it was as simply natural for one who honoured them both to do honest homage, before and after they had left us, to the saintly and secluded poetess as to the adventurous and unsaintly hero. Wherever anything is worthy of honour and thanksgiving it is or it always should be as natural if not as delightful to give thanks and do honour to a stranger as to a friend, to a benefactor long since dead as to a benefactor still alive. To the kindred spirits of Philip Sidney and Aurelio Saffi it was almost as equal a pleasure to offer what tribute I could bring as if Sidney also could have honoured me with his personal friendship. To Tennyson and Browning it was no less fit that I should give honour than that I should do homage to the memory of Bruno, the martyred friend of Sidney. And I can hardly remember any task that I ever took more delight in discharging than I felt in the inadequate and partial payment of a lifelong debt to the marvellous and matchless succession of poets who made the glory of our country incomparable for ever by the work they did between the joyful date of the rout of the Armada and the woful date of the outbreak of civil war.

Charles Lamb, as I need not remind you, wrote for antiquity:

nor need you be assured that when I write plays it is with a view to
their being acted at the Globe, the Red Bull, or the Black Friars.
And whatever may be the dramatic or other defects of "Marino
Faliero" or "Locrine," they do certainly bear the same relation
to previous plays or attempts at plays on the same subjects as
"King Henry V." to "The Famous Victories"—if not as "King
Lear," a poem beyond comparison with all other works of man
except possibly "Prometheus" and "Othello," to the primitive
and infantile scrawl or drivel of "King Leir and his three daughters." The fifth act of "Marino Faliero," hopelessly impossible
as it is from the point of view of modern stagecraft, could hardly
have been found too untheatrical, too utterly given over to talk
without action, by the audiences which endured and applauded the
magnificent monotony of Chapman's eloquence—the fervent and
inexhaustible declamation which was offered and accepted as a
substitute for study of character and interest of action when his
two finest plays, if plays they can be called, found favour with
an incredibly intelligent and an inconceivably tolerant audience.
The metrical or executive experiment attempted and carried
through in "Locrine" would have been improper to any but a
purely and wholly romantic play or poem: I do not think that the
life of human character or the lifelikeness of dramatic dialogue
has suffered from the bondage of rhyme or has been sacrificed to
the exigence of metre. The tragedy of "The Sisters," however
defective it may be in theatrical interest or progressive action, is
the only modern English play I know in which realism in the
reproduction of natural dialogue and accuracy in the representa-
tion of natural intercourse between men and women of gentle
birth and breeding have been found or made compatible with
expression in genuine if simple blank verse. It is not for me to
decide whether anything in the figures which play their parts on
my imaginary though realistic stage may be worthy of sympathy,
attention, or interest: but I think they talk and act as they would
have done in life without ever lapsing into platitude or breaking
out of nature.

In "Rosamund, Queen of the Lombards," I took up a subject
long since mishandled by an English dramatist of all but the
highest rank, and one which in later days Alfieri has commem-

orated in a magnificent passage of a wholly unhistoric and somewhat unsatisfactory play. The comparatively slight deviation from historic records in the final catastrophe or consummation of mine is not, I think, to say the least, injurious to the tragic effect or the moral interest of the story.

A writer conscious of any natural command over the musical resources of his language can hardly fail to take such pleasure in the enjoyment of this gift or instinct as the greatest writer and the greatest versifier of our age must have felt at its highest possible degree when composing a musical exercise of such incomparable scope and fullness as "Les Djinns." But if he be a poet after the order of Hugo or Coleridge or Shelley, the result will be something very much more than a musical exercise; though indeed, except to such ears as should always be kept closed against poetry, there is no music in verse which has not in it sufficient fullness and ripeness of meaning, sufficient adequacy of emotion or of thought, to abide the analysis of any other than the purblind scrutiny of prepossession or the squint-eyed inspection of malignity. There may perhaps be somewhat more depth and variety of feeling or reflection condensed into the narrow frame of the poems which compose "A Century of Roundels" than would be needed to fulfil the epic vacuity of a Chœrilus or a Coluthus. And the form chosen for my only narrative poem was chosen as a test of the truth of my conviction that such work could be done better on the straitest and the strictest principles of verse than on the looser and more slippery lines of mediæval or modern improvisation. The impulsive and irregular verse which had been held sufficient for the stanza selected or accepted by Thornton and by Tennyson seemed capable of improvement and invigoration as a vehicle or a medium for poetic narrative. And I think it has not been found unfit to give something of dignity as well as facility to a narrative which recasts in modern English verse one of the noblest and loveliest old English legends. There is no episode in the cycle of Arthurian romance more genuinely Homeric in its sublime simplicity and its pathetic sublimity of submission to the masterdom of fate than that which I have rather reproduced than recast in "The Tale of Balen": and impossible as it is to render the text or express the spirit of the Iliad in English prose or rhyme

—above all, in English blank verse—it is possible, in such a metre as was chosen and refashioned for this poem, to give some sense of the rage and rapture of battle for which Homer himself could only find fit and full expression by similitudes drawn like mine from the revels and the terrors and the glories of the sea.

It is nothing to me that what I write should find immediate or general acceptance: it is much to know that on the whole it has won for me the right to address this dedication and inscribe this edition to you.

ALGERNON CHARLES SWINBURNE.

Explanatory Notes

NOTES ON POEMS AND REVIEWS

17. As . . . face. John Webster, *The White Devil*, III. 2. 149–50.

18. Beasts at Ephesus. I Cor. 15:32.

18. "For . . . them." In Ben Jonson's "To the Reader," at the conclusion of *The Poetaster*.

18. Infusoria. The passage anticipates the stance of *Under the Microscope*.

18. "Especially horrible." Quoted from the *London Review*, XIII (August 4, 1866), 130.

19. A lump . . . bird-footed. Shelley's *The Witch of Atlas*, XI. 7–8.

19. *Ma corruption . . . pudeur.* The statement that "my depravity would blush at their modesty" neatly fits the context. If the French is a quotation, the source is undiscovered.

20. Catullus "translated." In Catullus, LI. Latin *traducere*, "to translate," also means "to misrepresent." Swinburne was fond of recalling the Italian equation of *traduttóre* and *traditóre*.

20. Ambrose Philips, as the name is usually written (*c.* 1675–1749) in "A Fragment from Sappho," and Nicolas Boileau-Despréaux (1636–1711) in *Traité du sublime*, chap. VIII, a translation of Longinus's treatise, are referred to here.

21. The Greek quotation is from the *Iliad*, IV. 43: "Of mine own will, yet with reluctant mind," cited by Swinburne himself as the equivalent of the Homeric phrase (Lang, IV, 230).

21. By the side. Swinburne's letter to W. M. Rossetti of October 13, 1866, mentions his wish to change to this reading (Lang, I, 200).

21. "All air and fire." Michael Drayton's phrase in regard to Marlowe, in his "To My Most Dearly-Loved Friend Henry Reynolds, Esquire, of Poets and Poesy."

22. "Violent . . . ends." *Romeo and Juliet*, II. vi. 9.

22. The quotations are from Shelley's *Queen Mab*, VII. 164, 172, 180. Moxon and Co., the publishers of *Queen Mab*, published *Poems and Ballads* before it was transferred to Hotten.

23. Moods . . . worth. Matthew Arnold, "To a Gypsy Child by the Seashore," line 18.

Boldface numbers refer to pages of the text.

23. Cotytto. A Thracian goddess the nature of whose rites suggests identification with the originally Phrygian Cybele.

23. Origen (185–254), important Christian theologian, is mentioned as a type of the religious eunuch along with the mythical Atys, who, driven mad by the mother-goddess Cybele, emasculated himself (Swinburne knew the account in Catullus, LXIII). The corybantes and priests of Cybele also became eunuchs.

23. On Dindymus, a mountain in Phrygia, stood an early sanctuary of Cybele. In Loreto, in central Italy, was a church reputed to contain the Virgin's house, originally in Nazareth but said to have been brought thence by angels. At one time Loreto was regarded as "the Christian Mecca."

23. "Islands of the blest" was used by Byron (*Don Juan*, III. 700), in the poem beginning, "The isles of Greece . . . ." Byron's editors cite the Greek for "the blessed isles" (Hesiod's *Works and Days*, line 171), interpreted as the Cape Verde islands or the Canaries. The name Hesperia was of course used for the western land, Italy, in Vergil's *Aeneid*, III. 163.

24. The French for "Who has drunk will drink" is apparently proverbial.

24. Euphrasy and rue. Cf. *Paradise Lost*, XI. 414.

24. "Is . . . it." *The Book of Common Prayer* gives this reading for Psalm 139:6.

24. Théophile Gautier, *Albertus*, XCVIII: "I warn the mothers of families that I am not writing for little girls, for whom one makes bread and butter; my verses are a young man's verses."

25. MM. Purgon and Diafoirus are characters in Molière's *Le Malade imaginaire*.

26. The elder Faustina was the wife of the Emperor Antoninus Pius and the mother of the younger Faustina, who married her cousin Marcus Aurelius. Legend is less kind to the characters of the two women than sober history.

26. Foolish virgins. Matt. 25:1 ff.

26. The fallen goddess . . . divine. See, for instance, *Œuvres complètes de Charles Baudelaire*, ed. M. Jacques Crepet (Paris, 1925), II, 215–16, 220, 226.

28. In Plato . . . absurd. In the *Symposium*.

28. More than once ". . . sculptor's love." Though the phrasing quoted by Swinburne has not been found in Shelley, both *The Witch of Atlas* and "Lines Connected with Epipsychidion" refer to "that sweet marble monster of both sexes." Chapter IX of Gautier's *Mademoiselle de Maupin*, a work Swinburne greatly admired, has much to say of the ancient piece of sculpture.

28. The words quoted are, of course, from the first line of Keats's *Endymion*; the following words sound like a reminiscence from the "Ode on a Grecian Urn," line 26: "For ever warm and still to be enjoy'd."

28. The phrases "loathsome and horrible," "nameless and abominable," and "unspeakable foulnesses" were used in John Morley's unsigned critique of *Poems and Ballads* in the *Saturday Review*, XXII (August 4, 1866), 145–47.

29. "However . . . *me*." From Landor's "Appendix to the *Hellenics*," *Poems*, ed. Stephen Wheeler (London, 1935), III (*Complete Works*, XV), 236, lines 47–48.

29. In *A Swinburne Library*, p. 32, Wise quotes "the lines as Swinburne first wrote them":

A Query

Why should you grudge me lyre and laurel,
  O toothless mouth, O soundless maw?
I never grudged you bell and coral,
  I never grudged you troughs and straw.

Lie still in kennel, snug in stable,
  Good creatures of the stall or sty;
Shove snouts for crumbs beneath the table;
  Lie still; and rise not up to lie.

30. Ariosto (1474–1533), the great Italian poet most renowned for *Orlando Furioso*, "laughs in the sun"; Aretino (1492–1556), some of whose works are obscene, "sniggers in the shade." Though the antithesis seems characteristic of Hugo's style, the lines have not been found in Hugo or other French authors.

30. The whiter . . . within. Cf. Matt. 23:27.

30. "It . . . sound." From Ben Jonson's song from *Epicœne, or The Silent Woman* (Act I, scene 1) beginning, "Still to be neat, still to be dressed."

31. "Line" refers to standard of life or course of conduct.

31. The *O. E. D.* cites Carlyle's *Miscellanies* as using "gig-man" in the sense of "one whose respectability is measured by his keeping a gig; . . . a 'Philistine'."

Swinburne's description fitted poems like Buchanan's "Liz" and "Nell," and Buchanan considered the passage aimed at him. But was it? One might with equal plausibility suppose that in referring to "idyls of the . . . deanery" Swinburne was thinking of Patmore's *Angel in the House*. Since

other poems, now forgotten, may have fitted descriptions like this or
"idyls of the gutter and the gibbet," one must distinguish between suspicion and certainty.

31. House . . . feasting. Cf. Eccl. 7:2.

31. I . . . height. From Landor's *Poems,* ed. Wheeler, III (*Collected
Works,* XV), 277, in "Poems on Books and Writers."

UNDER THE MICROSCOPE

35. Though . . . angels. Cf. I Cor. 13:1.

35. The etymology of *malaria* (Italian *mala aria*) implies the mythical
connection between malaria and bad air.

36. Many mansions . . . house. Cf. John 14:2.

36. "In . . . room." Pope, *Moral Essays,* III. 299.

37. For Blake's "ghost of a flea," see the concluding paragraphs of
chap. XXVIII of Alexander Gilchrist's *Life of William Blake.*

Armande Marie de Pontmartin (1811–1890) is remembered for attacks
on men of letters.

37. "Where Orpheus . . . are." Matthew Arnold's "Resignation," line
208.

37. "Killed . . . critique" is quoted from Byron's *Don Juan,* canto 11,
LIX, in reference to Keats. For Carlyle's remark, in "Boswell's Life of
Johnson," see *Critical and Miscellaneous Essays,* III (London, 1899), 116.

38. Except for the deified Mrs. Grundy, the actors, whose names derive
mostly from the *commedia dell' arte,* are introduced in relation to the
Quarterly Review, long notorious for attacks on eminent authors.

39. ". . . an intruder who has climbed into the sheepfold!" seems
reminiscent of Milton's *Lycidas,* line 115, "Creep, and intrude, and climb
into the fold!" For "to tremble with Felix," cf. Acts 24:25.

39. A review of Karl Elze's *Lord Byron* (Berlin, 1870), with the
running head "Byron and Tennyson," now attributed to Abraham Hayward, appeared in the *Quarterly Review,* CXXXI (October, 1871), 354–
92.

39. Awful . . . lovely. *Paradise Lost,* IV. 847–48.

39. "So familiar . . . society." Quoted from Hayward's remarks, pp.
381–82.

39. The *Quarterly Review* praised Byron's episode of Don Juan among
young women, though, as the poet says (*Don Juan,* canto 6, XLII), "A
kind of sleepy Venus seem'd Dudù." For Hayward's comments on "The
Sisters," see the *Quarterly Review,* CXXXI (October, 1871), 379.

40. With "not convenient," cf. Eph. 5:4: "Neither filthiness, nor foolish talking, nor jesting, which are not convenient." "Well stricken in years" is from Luke 1:7, 18, and "unspotted from the world" from Jas. 1:27.

40. Regarding the hypothesis that Swinburne composed the French (and possibly the English) verses to fit the context, see p. 12. A translation of the French follows:

"Sire, your austere spirit is a chosen spirit: Now, when the human conscience has become bankrupt, your pure voice is like a bugle-call that one hears sounding from the depth of the shadow where destiny lies in wait for us. The naked craving, the famished and mocking flesh, bitter and degrading spring where unheeding youth drinks, the cynical lewdness with its wicked animal gaze hide, at the sight of you, like a dog in its kennel. Impure laughter never comes to defile with mud your lip where gleams the apostle's and the angel's fire. The hoarse-voiced satyr cowers beneath your glance; at your approach, vice, grown silent, trembles; and the snow that falls abundantly on your bent head, when one has caught a glimpse of your heart, no longer seems white."

40. "Hoarse-voiced satyr" refers to "Le satyre au chant rauque," whereas "the depth of ill-breeding and bad taste" is quoted from Hayward's discussion of *The Princess* (see above, fourth note to p. 39).

42. Hayward's review of Rossetti's *Poems*, Swinburne's *Songs before Sunrise*, and Morris's *The Earthly Paradise* in the *Quarterly Review*, CXXXII (January, 1872), 59–84, contains the phrases Swinburne quotes: "No terms . . . sexual relation," "gross profanity," and "emasculate obscenity." Hayward says of Rossetti's *Poems*, "Mysteries of this sort are intelligible enough, but they belong to the worship of no deity but Priapus."

"Terrible voice . . . judgment" is unidentified.

42. For "the honest garden-god" see the note on the verse quoted on p. 71 (below, p. 119).

42. Satiric essay . . . Gautier. Gautier's preface to *Mademoiselle de Maupin*.

42. From the *Quarterly Review*, CXXXII (January, 1872), 66: "We are in doubt whether to blame him [Swinburne] most for his want of decency or want of sense."

43. "Know . . . hand." *Twelfth Night*, III. iv. 31.

43. A god . . . believe. From the *Quarterly Review*, CXXXII (January, 1872), 65: "What, then, is the meaning of all this vapouring against a Being who is believed to be a nonentity?"

43. A great poetess . . . dead. Mrs. Browning in "The Dead Pan."

43. A reference to the war of the cranes and pigmies, which became a theme in Greek art, occurs in Homer. The pseudo-Homeric *Batrachomyomachia* describes the battle of the frogs and mice.

44. "The skunk . . . approach." From Macaulay's essay on Leigh Hunt's edition of Wycherley, Congreve, Vanbrugh, and Farquhar (Everyman's Library Edition of the *Essays,* p. 435).

44. Cf. Shakespeare's *Pericles,* I. i. 64–65:

> "I am no viper, yet I feed
> On mother's flesh which did me breed."

45. John Oldmixon (1673–1742) and Edmund Curll (1675–1747), both critics of Pope, were ridiculed in Pope's *Dunciad.*

45. In referring to Whiston and Ditton Swinburne has in mind verses not now accepted as Swift's. See Lang, III, 219, note 4.

45. A noted libeller. *Johnsoniana* . . . (London, 1836), p. 116, ascribes the anecdote, concerning Foote, to Sir John Hawkins.

45. "With . . . hand." Coleridge, "To a Friend [Charles Lamb] Who Had Declared His Intention of Writing No More Poetry," line 35.

45. "Pass without looking" seems reminiscent of Dante's *Inferno,* III. 51: "Non ragioniam di lor, ma guarda e passa."
The Marquis de Mascarille and the Vicomte de Jodelet are valets who pose as noblemen, in Molière's *Les Précieuses ridicules.*

45. Nothing . . . critical. Cf. *Othello,* II. i. 120: "For I am nothing, if not critical."

45. Such a Nazarene generation. Cf. John 1:46: "Can there any good thing come out of Nazareth?"

46. The quotation from Hugo's *"Querelles du sérail"* (*Les Châtiments,* III. 5) mentions the wars of the animalcule with the bacterium in a drop of water.

46. "The . . . jars." Cf. the first two lines of Tennyson's "Literary Squabbles":

> "Ah God! the petty fools of rhyme
> That shriek and sweat in pigmy wars" (not "jars").

47. "Injured merit" is from *Paradise Lost,* I. 98.

47. "Pestered . . . nature." *Troilus and Cressida,* V. i. 38–39.

48. The "monitor" is Abraham Hayward.

48. "Blind mouths." *Lycidas,* line 119.

48. Look here . . . presentment. *Hamlet,* III. iv. 53–54.

49. In *The Poetry of the Period* (pp. 269–72) Austin discusses "The Poet's Mind." Cf. p. 9.

49. For Landor's parody of Byron's "By the Rivers of Babylon We

Sat Down and Wept," see *Poems,* ed. Wheeler, III (*Complete Works,* XV), 258.

49. John Hopkins (*c.* 1520–1570) collaborated with Thomas Stern-hold, and Nicholas Brady (1659–1726) with Nahum Tate, on metrical versions of the Psalms.

49. The "Lotus-eaters." Correctly, "The Lotos-Eaters."

49. Austin's *Poetry of the Period* quotes stanzas XCII–XCIII and XCVI–XCVII of the third canto of *Childe Harold's Pilgrimage,* thus omitting two stanzas.

50. William Hayley (1745–1820), mediocre poet and friend and biographer of William Cowper, was satirized by Byron in *English Bards and Scotch Reviewers,* lines 310–18.

50. "Is . . . Ruin?" Shelley's "Mont Blanc," lines 71–73.

50. "If . . . well." In *Absalom and Achitophel,* Part II, lines 419–20, Doeg, who represents Elkanah Settle (1648–1724), is said to have

"fagoted his notions as they fell,
And if they rhym'd and rattled, all was well."

51. In the Introduction to *A Selection from the Works of Lord Byron* (1866), reprinted in *Essays and Studies,* Swinburne "elsewhere" had dis-cussed Byron.

51. *Quis vituperavit?* "Who has censured?"

51. From the tribe of Levi, a son of Jacob, came the priesthood, here linked with hypocrites professing religion, like Molière's Tartuffe.

51. "Blatant . . . Massachusetts" alludes to Harriet Beecher Stowe, christened by the poet "Mrs. Bitcher Spewe" (Lang, IV, 140). Claiming to have based it largely on Lady Byron's confidences, in 1869 Mrs. Stowe shocked the literary world with a sensational magazine article, "The True Story of Lady Byron's Life." Cf. above, p. 9.

51. "Ubi . . . agitant." "Where with shrill yells they shake the holy emblems" (Catullus, LXIII. 24; Loeb Classical Library edition, tr. F. W. Cornish).

52. The Floralia, the ancient festival of Flora, Roman goddess of flowers, came to include indecent performances and games.

52. The Biblical phrasing in "naked and not ashamed" (cf. Gen. 2:25) and "infernal Pentecost" (cf. Acts 2:1 ff.) may be obvious, like the allusions to the ancient Eleusinian mysteries and to Celaeno, queen of the harpies, described by Vergil as woman-bird monsters with filthy habits (*Aeneid,* III. 210 ff.).

53. A boy . . . puddle. The *Saturday Review,* XXXI (January 14, 1871), 54–55, so described the author of *Songs before Sunrise.*

53. Shelley often links kings and priests, as in *Prometheus Unbound,*
III. iv. 173.

54. No ear . . . long. Swinburne perhaps recalls Midas's poor ear for
music. After Midas indicated belief in Pan's musical superiority to Apollo,
the latter changed Midas's human to ass's ears, as told by Ovid (*Meta-
morphoses,* XI. 146 ff.).

54. Shriek . . . himself. After mentioning Swinburne's statement that
Byron could not sing, Austin answers: "He means a singer who did not
and would not screech, as poor Shelley now and then unfortunately did;
and who positively *could not* indulge in those falsetto notes which appear
to compose most of Mr. Swinburne's emasculated poetical voice" (*The
Poetry of the Period,* p. 114).

54. Sir Hugh Evans ". . . ears." *Merry Wives of Windsor,* I. i. 150,
152.

54. "Qui . . . gens." *Critique de l'Ecole des femmes,* sc. 5. "Our Mar-
quises de Mascarille," after seeing a picture or hearing a concert, are said to
"blame and praise just in the same wrong-headed way. They pick up
shibboleths about art wherever they can, and never fail to mutilate and
misuse them. For Heaven's sakes, gentlemen, hold your tongues. If the
Almighty has not blessed you with the knowledge of anything, do not
make yourselves the laughing stock of those who listen to you, and
remember that, if you do not speak a word, you may possibly be taken
for clever people" (tr. R. D. Waller).

55. The stanza on Miltiades is in the "Isles of Greece" passage, in the
third canto of *Don Juan.*

55. "A . . . hit." *Hamlet,* V. ii. 292.

57. Less sinned . . . sinning. Cf. *King Lear,* III. ii. 59–60: "More
sinned against than sinning."

57. According to the *D. N. B.,* during a visit to Paris Abraham Hayward became acquainted with Louis Adolphe Thiers (1797–1877), states-
man and historian, and the two men afterward carried on correspondence.

57. A work by Alexandre Dumas *fils* (1824–1895), *La Dame aux
camélias,* has as its central character a courtesan, portrayed sympathetically
both in the earlier novel and in the author's later dramatized version.
Swinburne's " 'camelias' " refers to similar stories.

"Camelias," like Swinburne's "transcendant" (p. 69), perhaps illus-
trates the French influence on his spelling, though a better illustration
would be the "correspondance" frequent in his letters.

58. Tennyson more than once used the phrase "blameless king" of
King Arthur, and the Laureate's implied analogy between his hero and
Prince Albert was a recurring source of hilarity to Swinburne.

58. "Man at all." Cf. Tennyson's *Merlin and Vivien,* line 779 (Student's Cambridge Edition).

59. "The curse denounced on parricide" recalls the story of Oedipus, also guilty of incest, but "mere casual indulgence of light love and passing wantonness" should be associated with "the incestuous birth of Mordred from the connexion of Arthur with his half-sister, unknowing and unknown," previously mentioned.

59. Ate was first personified as a divinity in Homer's *Iliad,* representing a kind of infatuation and moral blindness leading to ruin; ultimately a punisher of unrighteous actions. Cf. the passage from Aeschylus quoted below.

59. "The great old book" is the *Morte D'Arthur,* by Sir Thomas Malory (as the name is now usually spelled).

59. Aeschylus, *Choephoroi,* 1075–76: "Oh when will it work its accomplishment, when will the fury of calamity [Ate], lulled to rest, find an end and cease?" (Loeb Classical Library, tr. Herbert Weir Smyth).

59. On the canceled passage, see the variants in the textual notes and above, p. 9.

59. *Merlin and Vivien,* line 744 (Swinburne's italics).

60. "As . . . street." *Ibid.,* line 796.

60. Dalilah. "Dalila" in *Samson Agonistes,* the "Delilah" of the King James Bible.

60. Phraxanor was Potiphar's wife in the drama *Joseph and His Brethren,* by Charles J. Wells, who died in 1879.

60. "Smiling saucily." *Merlin and Vivien,* lines 266, 649.

60. "The end . . . death." Cf. Rom. 6:21: "For the end of those things is death."

60. "Fulgurant." Cf. Charles Asselineau, *"Charles Baudelaire: sa vie et son oeuvre,"* in *Baudelaire et Asselineau* (Paris, 1953), p. 120.

60. Swinburne refers to lines 423–30 of *"La Confiance du Marquis Fabrice,"* in *L'Italie—Ratbert* (Hugo's *La Légende des siècles*).

60. "Saucy." Quoted in allusion to Vivien.

61. The tawny blonde mentioned on this page is Matha (cf. line 428 of Hugo's poem just mentioned).

61. "In . . . fellows." Middleton and Rowley, *The Changeling,* III. iv (Mermaid Series, ed. Havelock Ellis, I, 129).

61. Captain Dugald Dalgetty, a character in Scott's *Legend of Montrose*—as he says, "Major in a regiment of loyal Irishes"—being proud of his learning, frequently introduces a sententious Latin quotation, though not this one: "Who gain profit not of the body but of the mind."

61. "What is 'Maud' about? Woman. What is 'The Princess' about?

Woman, woman. What are the four 'Idylls of the King' about? Woman, woman, woman, woman" (*The Poetry of the Period*, p. 96).

61. "Hardly . . . with." Austin says of Swinburne's character Chastelard: "I scarcely like to own sex with him" (*The Poetry of the Period*, p. 107).

61. "The Fleshly School of Poetry," the article by "Thomas Maitland," refers to "this protracted hankering" after "a person of the other sex" (*Contemporary Review*, XVIII [October, 1871], 343; cf. *The Fleshly School*, p. 45). In "Literary Morality," a chapter in *David Gray, and Other Essays* (London, 1868), reprinted from the *Fortnightly Review*, VI (September 15, 1866), 289–300, Buchanan defended the sincerity—hence the "morality"—of Petronius Arbiter, though some characters in the *Satyricon* display homosexual tendencies.

62. In *The Luck of an Autograph Collector* (Washington, D.C., 1950), John S. Mayfield reproduced a letter in which Burroughs declared, "I have no explanation to offer of how he came to daub [*sic*] me Dr." Burroughs penciled a similar statement beneath Swinburne's note on "Dr. Burroughs' excellent little book" (above, p. 64) in a copy of *Under the Microscope* that Mr. Mayfield acquired.

62. One thing . . . needful indeed. Cf. Luke 10:42: "But one thing is needful."

63. *Solvitur ambulando.* "The difficulty is solved by walking," just as "the proof of the pudding" is a test by eating. Perhaps in this respect comparable to Doctor Johnson's stamping on the ground in order to disprove Bishop Berkeley's assumption that matter is mental, the saying has been thought pertinent to an ancient philosophical-mathematical difficulty about motion: if the latter is capable of indefinite subdivision, how could one person ever pass another?

63. *Si . . . est.* "If that is of any consequence."

64. Twenty-four letters. Not all American students know that in the older English alphabet two pairs of letters, *i* and *j* and *u* and *v*, are treated respectively as one letter rather than as two.

64. The "little book" is John Burroughs' *Notes on Walt Whitman as Poet and Person* (New York, 1867). As indicated below, Swinburne also knew the second "edition," or later issue (New York, 1871).

64. Athanasius (*c.* 295–373), Bishop of Alexandria, four times exiled, was often in the position of opposing the world. His opposition to the Arian heresy became orthodox. Though Whitman's poetic faith and practice seemed heterodox, his followers believed them correct—just as if he had been Athanasius.

64. Burroughs writes (p. 69): "In the grand literary relics of nations

it may be observed that their best poetry has always spurned the routine poetic, and adopted essentially the prose form, preserving interior rhythm only." Swinburne adds italics to the passage he quotes from the "German" writer (Burroughs, p. 70).

65. "I . . . ardour for them." Quoted from Burroughs' *Notes* of 1871, p. 119, containing some material not in the early volume.

65. In his *Notes* (p. 69) Burroughs writes of "the dulcet metres of Tennyson."

65. "An outward . . . grace." From the Catechism in *The Book of Common Prayer*.

66. Whitman's comments on "the Democratic requirements" being "insulted" in Shakespeare, on the superiority of Spanish literature, on Shakespeare as "the tally of Feudalism" and as "incarnated, uncompromising Feudalism, in literature," like the phrase "the British element," appear in the 1871 edition of *Democratic Vistas,* in the section on British literature, especially p. 81.

66. The reference is to Victor Hugo's son, the translator of Shakespeare.

68. A Thanksgiving Ode . . . cap. James Russell Lowell's "Ode Recited at the Harvard Commemoration, July 21, 1865."

68. The official odes by poets-laureate and others—hence the mention of Whitehall as a center of government—were thought of as Pindaric, particularly in the seventeenth century, when the structure of Pindar's odes was not generally understood. Pindar was from Thebes.

68. "An ignorant . . . at all." Quoted from *The Poetry of the Period,* p. 292. An unsigned review in the *Spectator* for September 11, 1869, contains (p. 1075) a passage from which Austin quotes. Swinburne evidently identified the reviewer as Buchanan.

68. "Hawks . . . een." *The Oxford Dictionary of Proverbs* cites from Scott's *Rob Roy* a proverb nearly identical.

68. The hymnologist. Cf. Isaac Watts's "Song XVII. Love Between Brother and Sister," in *Divine Songs for Children:*

> "Birds in their little nest agree;
> And 'tis a shameful sight,
> When children of one family
> Fall out, and chide, and fight."

68. The verse quoted by Boswell reads:

> "Peace, coxcombs, peace, and both agree,
> N——, kiss thy empty brother;
> Religion laughs at foes like thee,
> And dreads a friend like t'other."

69. Cf. Isaac Watts, cited above, "Song XVI. Against Quarrelling and Fighting":

> "But, children, you should never let
> Such angry passions rise;
> Your little hands were never made
> To tear each other's eyes."

69. With the passage quoted in Swinburne's note cf. W. S. Landor's "To Caina" (*Poems*, ed. Wheeler, IV [*Complete Works*, XVI], 302): "Is it that carts have lost their tails?"

The "eloquent essay" was of course Lowell's "On a Certain Condescension in Foreigners."

69. "AND . . . EYE." Swinburne knew that Lowell wrote this passage (in the third page under "Italy" in *Fireside Travels*). For his harsh comment on it in 1877 see Lang, III, 303.

70. In reality Ruskin describes Buchanan's "abuse" as "unmatchable . . . for obliquitous platitude in the mud-walks of literature" (*The Works of John Ruskin*, ed. Cook and Wedderburn, XXVII, 180).

70. The Greek is from Aeschylus, *Agamemnon*, lines 160–61: "Whosoever he be, if by this name it well pleaseth him to be invoked" (Loeb Classical Library, tr. Smyth).

70. "At the time of the publication [the *Contemporary Review* article on "The Fleshly School of Poetry"] I myself was yachting among the Scottish Hebrides," declares Buchanan's preface to *The Fleshly School of Poetry, and Other Phenomena of the Day* (London, 1872), p. v. See also p. 8, above.

70. "Holy Willie" is the hypocritical speaker in Burns's "Holy Willie's Prayer."

70. "This great city of civilisation" is from *The Fleshly School*, p. 2.

70. Buchanan indicates his "emulation" of Aeschylus in *The Drama of Kings* (London, 1871), terming the *Persae* "in some respects the very finest of the extant Greek tragedies" (p. 452). For the comment on Dante, see *The Fleshly School*, p. 11. Such poems as Baudelaire's Buchanan describes as "wearing to the brain" (*ibid.*, p. 77). For the two other passages from *The Fleshly School*, see pp. 82 and 86.

71. Horace calls Apollo *"Delius et Patareus Apollo"* (*Carm.* III. iv. 64). Patara, a city in Asia Minor, was a seat of the worship of Apollo, fabled to have been born on the island of Delos.

71. "Matutine . . . audis?" Horace, *Sermones*, II. vi. 20: "O father of the morning, or Janus, if you would prefer to be so addressed" (tr. H. W. Wells).

71. The quoted lines are from W. S. Landor, "Inscription on a Plinth in the Garden of Mnestheus at Lampsacus," in *Poems,* ed. Wheeler, IV (*Complete Works,* XVI), 169. Instead of "Beware!" Landor has, "Take heed unto your ways!"

71. At the end of *A Drama of Kings* (cf. note 113), Buchanan has "On Mystic Realism: A Note for the Adept," in which he calls his own work "the first serious attempt ever made to treat great contemporary events in a dramatic form and very realistically, yet with something of the massive grandeur of style characteristic of the great dramatists of Greece."

71. Swinburne has in mind the words spoken by Aphrodite in the Prologue to *Hippolytus,* lines 3 ff., but composes lines suitable to Buchanan: "Great among written works and not nameless, I am called a shady liar within the city; and to those who dwell beyond the limits of the Atlantic Ocean in island ships and who nourish me I give lip service as a flatterer, but those who spurn me I attack covertly." For this translation the editor is indebted to Professor L. R. Lind of the University of Kansas.

71. Lauder and Macpherson, if not introduced merely to create verisimilitude, are unidentified.

71. "The masters I fawn upon with slavish heart, but those who do not know me (Cod. Var. [variant MS reading], to whom I am unknown), etc."

71. "With . . . motives." "My article was altered and my name suppressed with the best of all motives" (p. vii) appears, like "the inventions of cowards" (p. v), in the preface to *The Fleshly School.*

72. From Aeschylus, *Choephoroi,* line 757: "Children's young inwards work their own relief" (Loeb Classical Library, tr. Smyth).

72. *Ibid.,* line 760: "Laundress [Swinburne's " 'fuller' "] and nurse had the same office."

72. Shakespeare's Doll Tearsheet and Buchanan's Nell have a common occupation.

72. La Fontaine, *Fables,* V. iii. "The little fish will get big provided God grants him life."

72. In the Aesopic fable "The Frog and the Ox," a frog tries to blow himself to an ox's size and bursts.

73. "The Fleshly School of Poetry" by "Thomas Maitland" alleged that Rossetti's "Jenny" had been suggested by Buchanan's own work. In "The Stealthy School of Criticism" (the *Athenaeum,* December 16, 1871, pp. 792–94) Rossetti denied any knowledge of Buchanan's poems. Nevertheless Buchanan repeated the remark in his pamphlet (p. 45).

73. "The intense . . . schoolmaster." From Buchanan's chapter "On My Own Tentatives," in *David Gray, and Other Essays,* especially p. 308.

73. Most of the comments appear in *David Gray, and Other Essays:* "Yet Shakespeare is occasionally as gross as any of his contemporaries; while Jonson, an inferior writer, through a straightforward and splendid nature, is singularly pure" (p. 260). "Mr. Carlyle, as we have seen, preaches brutalism in language as harsh as the barking of Cerberus" (*ibid.,* p. 193; cf. p. 186). "Thackeray was not quite so wise [as Scott], being a so much smaller writer and inferior artist; he worked in his own sickening and peculiar fashion . . ." (p. 263). In "Tennyson's Charm," *Saint Pauls Magazine,* X (1872), 282–303, Buchanan calls Shelley "hysterical" (p. 284) and refers to Landor's "woodenheadedness," Keats's "hectic excitement," and Shelley's "hysteria" (p. 285).

73. "Gentleman parcel-poet." *The Poetaster,* IV. vi. 29 (*The Works of Ben Jonson,* ed. Herford and Simpson, IV, 281).

74. From *The Poetaster,* III. i. 243–45: "Let me not live, but I think thou and I . . . shall lift them all out of favour, both Virgil, Varius, and the best of them" (Herford and Simpson, IV, 241).

74. "Do but . . . than I." *The Poetaster,* III. i. 160–67 (Herford and Simpson, IV, 239).

74. The dog . . . vomit. Prov. 26:11.

74. "Divers and sundry calumnies." *The Poetaster,* V. iii. 413 (Herford and Simpson, IV, 310).

74. "Or any . . . friends." *The Poetaster,* V. iii. 596–600 (Herford and Simpson, IV, 316).

74. "Motley . . . hand." Browning's *Sordello,* line 30.

74. ". . . his [Arnold's] utterance becomes the merest prose" (*David Gray, and Other Essays,* p. 296). Buchanan writes of Milton's "bald and turgid prose" (*ibid.,* p. 45). For other depreciatory comments on Milton see pp. 44, 46.

76. In his remarks on "the fleshly school," Buchanan severely criticized affectations of diction, especially Rossetti's. See also the article in *St. Pauls Magazine,* X (1872), especially 297–98, cited above.

76. Friendship of Landor and Southey, according to Byron, "will probably be as memorable as his own epics which (as I quoted to him ten or twelve years ago in 'English Bards') Porson said could be remembered when Homer and Virgil are forgotten, and not till then" (quoted in a note to the Appendix of *The Two Foscari; Letters and Journals,* ed. R. E. Prothero, VI, 389).

76. "A gifted young contemporary, who seems fond of throwing stones in my direction, fiercely upbraids me for writing 'Idylls of the gallows and the gutter,' and singing songs of 'costermongers and their trulls.' " (*David Gray, and Other Essays*, p. 291.)

77. Flattering unction . . . soul. Cf. *Hamlet*, III. iv. 145.

77. "Hart of grice" is Swinburne's phrase for "hart of grease," or "fat hart."

77. "Very soothing." As pointed out in Lang (II, 93 note), this favorite phrase of Swinburne's is spoken by Mr. Pecksniff, in *Martin Chuzzlewit*, chap. 9.

77. Aeschylus' *Choephoroi*, line 204: "From a little seed may spring a mighty stock" (Loeb Classical Library, tr. Smyth).

77. Fool . . . bent. Cf. *Hamlet*, III. ii. 401.

77. A neck-verse is ordinarily a verse from the Bible used to test the ability to read of those trying to save their necks by claiming benefit of clergy. Here Swinburne uses the expression in reference to Buchanan's verses concerned with a character sentenced to be hanged.

77. "Hangman's hands." *Macbeth*, II. ii. 28.

77. Named as mediocre poets are Wentworth Dillon, fourth Earl of Roscommon (*c.* 1633–1685); John Sheffield, third Earl of Mulgrave (1648–1721); Anne Finch, Countess of Winchilsea (1661–1720); Stephen Duck (1705–1756), Robert Bloomfield (1766–1823), and Mrs. Ann Yearsley (1756–1806).

78. "Grate . . . straw." *Lycidas*, line 124.

79. As early as Bacon's *Essays*, "a person of quality" meant a person of rank or social position.

79. "Is . . . too." The Irish bull is comparable to an "unknown American saying" as recorded in F. P. A.'s *Book of Quotations:* "I am just as good as you are, and a damned sight better."

79. What did Shelley . . . poor? Swinburne refers to an article by R. St. John Tyrwhitt, "The Immoral Theory of Art," *Contemporary Review*, V (August, 1867), 418–36, in a series, "Ancilla Domini: Thoughts on Christian Art."

79. The name Swinburne does not mention is of course that of Mazzini. For " 'seems' " in the following sentence see above, third note to p. 76.

80. Left hand . . . doing. Cf. Matt. 6:3.

80. In relation to what follows see textual note 60: A review of Buchanan's *Napoleon Fallen: A Lyrical Drama* in the *Athenaeum* (January 7, 1871, pp. 9–10), mentioned "rhymes in Swinburnian swing" in one chorus. *Napoleon Fallen* became part of a larger work, *The Drama of Kings*, whose reviewer in the same magazine (November 25, 1871), p. 683, identified Swinburne as the writer "on whom Mr. Buchanan is most clearly modelled." He adds, "And indeed Mr. Buchanan reminds us of

Mr. Swinburne in more ways than one." Even if Swinburne had overlooked such remarks, his own observations of literary resemblances might have led him to insert in the manuscript the passage which he finally decided to omit. The innuendo is unmistakable.

81. Buchanan's article in the *Contemporary Review* for October, 1871 (p. 338), dwells on "the Mutual Admiration School," and his pamphlet of 1872 charges that Rossetti, Morris, and Swinburne decried the work of others. Hayward's *Quarterly Review* article on the poetry of the three men (January, 1872, cited above) refers to them as "members of a mutual admiration society." "Coterie Glory" from the *Saturday Review* of February 24, 1872, is quoted in *The Fleshly School,* pp. 94–95.

82. Sub-leonine class. Swinburne is responding to what Buchanan had said of the "sub-Tennysonian school" in the works cited in the preceding note.

82. "Spurn . . . way." Cf. *Julius Caesar,* III. i. 46.

82. Joseph Surface and Seth Pecksniff are two famous hypocrites, one from Sheridan's *School for Scandal* and the other from Dickens' *Martin Chuzzlewit.*

82. As Ovid relates, Deucalion, the classical Noah, after a flood destroying the race created man anew by casting stones behind him.

83. Buchanan's letter in the *Athenaeum* (December 16, 1871, p. 794) that admitted authorship of the article signed "Thomas Maitland," a letter that followed one from Strahan and Company, publisher of the *Contemporary Review,* seeking to brush aside the notion that Buchanan wrote the article, contained this statement: "Mr. Strahan, publisher of the *Contemporary Review,* can corroborate me thus far, as he is best aware of the *inadvertence* [italics added] which led to the suppression of my own name." Even in the preface to *The Fleshly School* Buchanan, who referred to his yachting among the Hebrides, sought to excuse his having used an assumed name. In its review of *The Fleshly School,* the *Athenaeum* (May 25, 1872, pp. 650–51) stated: ". . . the suppression of Mr. Buchanan's name, so far from being the result of any 'inadvertence' whatever, had been due to his own express motion and desire, urgently reiterated from a distance and at the last moment" (p. 650).

83. "Judaeus Apella may believe it" ("Not I," Horace adds; *Sermones,* I. 5. 100). Swinburne's quoting "idyl" and "legend" is in allusion to Buchanan's *Idyls and Legends of Inverburn.*

83. The quotation humorously parallels a passage in the account of Elijah Pogram's levee in *Martin Chuzzlewit,* chap. XXIV.

83. In the "old couplet" Swinburne is adapting lines aimed at his friend G. A. Sala by James Hannay (1827–1873):

"S. steals from ev'ry modern author's page:
Yet in some circles S. is quite the rage.
'A man of talent, S.,' they all agree;
'A man of letters;' yes, a man of three."

—from the *Idler*,

I (1856), 151; quoted in George J. Worth, *James Hannay: His Life and Works* (Lawrence, Kansas, 1964), p. 71.

Swinburne suggests that the narrow range of "Crispinus" ("a man of three")—a name ultimately derived from Horace's satires and used, as previously indicated, by Ben Jonson in *The Poetaster*—may be illustrated by his misunderstanding of the Horatian *"domus exilis Plutonia"* (*Carm.*, I. 4. 17), in regard to the comfortless (*exilis*) dwelling of Pluto, as "a Plutonian house of exiles" (cited from *David Gray, and Other Essays*, p. 130).

In *The Drama of Kings* Buchanan included an "Epilude" at the end, after an "Epilogue." Hence Swinburne's reference to him as "a writer of 'epiludes.'"

83. George Buchanan (1506–1582) was an accomplished Latinist, whose tract *De jure regni* (according to the *D. N. B.*, familiar to members of the Long Parliament) is a dialogue between Buchanan and Thomas Maitland. That the association between the names may have led Buchanan to his choice of pseudonym is a possibility that has suggested itself independently to more than one person, including the present editor. "Contemporary," perhaps derisively echoing Buchanan's use of the word (see p. 76, above), refers to "the Tichborne claimant," Arthur Orton, in 1872 chief figure of a *cause célèbre*, who was found guilty of fraudulently claiming to be the missing heir of the Tichborne estate.

84. "The deep . . . Latinity." Buchanan's *David Gray, and Other Essays*, p. 247. The most attractive part of the *Satyricon* is the account of "the banquet of Trimalchio."

84. "The shallow . . . Prometheus." Quoted from *The Drama of Kings*, p. 455. For Buchanan's opinion of the *Persae*, see above, sixth note to p. 70.

85. Swinburne remembers Buchanan's remarks about Greek in "On My Own Tentatives" (especially pp. 291–93 and 314–17 of *David Gray, and Other Essays*).

85. The Latin phrase is quoted from Vergil's *Aeneid*, IV. 215: "with effeminate troop."

85. Hercules' enjoying in one night the fifty daughters of Thespius, a Boeotian king who wished to have grandchildren by him, was, according to Lempriere's *Classical Dictionary*, "the 13th and most arduous of the labors of Hercules."

85. With the lines quoted cf. Shakespeare's *Henry VIII*, II. 3. 41–42:

"I would not be a young count in your way,
For more than blushing comes to."

85. Swinburne thinks of the shirt of Nessus here because of its association with Hercules, who shot the centaur Nessus with a poisoned arrow when he tried to run away with Hercules' wife—a story with a tragic sequel.

85. *The Land of Lorne* was a book by Buchanan (1871), only partly concerned with the land around Oban—"some forty miles in length and fifteen in breadth," as he defines the district of Lorne.

86. Because of his pronouncements on Homer, Zoilus (*fl.* fourth century B. C.) is memorable for captious criticism. Thomas Rymer (1641–1713) achieved notoriety by harsh remarks on Shakespeare.

86. Pierre François Guyot, Abbé Desfontaines (1685–1745), and his disciple, Élie Fréron (1718–1766), partly because of their attacks on Voltaire have been regarded by subsequent French authors as petty critics.

86. "M. Veuillot, wittily, calls you a pumpkinhead"—line 99 of "Juillet, I. Les Deux Voix," in Hugo's *L'Année terrible*. Louis Veuillot (1813–1883), a French journalist known even in England for extreme ultramontane views, was a constant object of Hugo's aversion.

86. Lowell's critical estimate of Swinburne, chiefly of *Atalanta in Calydon,* appeared in the *North American Review,* CII (April, 1866), 544–55 (reprinted as "Swinburne's Tragedies" in *My Study Windows*). Lowell emphasizes the imitative nature of Swinburne's assimilation of the classical style in *Atalanta* and describes the author of *Chastelard* as reproducing "in his copy-book, more or less travestied, the copy that has been set for him at the page's head by the authors he most admires."

The subject of Swinburne's "Father Garasse" (included in *New Writings by Swinburne,* ed. Cecil Y. Lang), Garasse, a priest, was the persecutor of Théophile de Viau (1596–1626), a French poet Swinburne admired and wrote about (see the Bonchurch Edition, XIII). Claude-François Nonnotte (1711–1793), a minister, was a persistent critic of Voltaire. The name of Richard Flecknoe (died 1678?), the butt of a satire by Marvell, is less obscure because Dryden's satire on Shadwell is called *Mac Flecknoe.* John Dennis (1657–1734), an undistinguished critic, quarreled with, and was satirized by, Alexander Pope. Tribulation Wholesome, "a pastor of Amsterdam," is a satirical character in Ben Jonson's *Alchemist;* Zeal-of-the-Land Busy, a hypocritical Puritan in his *Bartholomew Fayre.*

87. Wears . . . head. Cf. *As You Like It,* II. i. 13.

87. Newt . . . toad. Cf. *A Midsummer-Night's Dream,* II. ii. 11; *Timon of Athens,* IV. iii. 182.

87. The old serpent. Cf. Gen. 3:13: "The serpent beguiled me, and I did eat," and Rev. 12:9 (cf. 20:2): "the old serpent called the Devil, and Satan."

87. With the phrasing of the last sentence cf. Gen. 3:14: ". . . upon thy belly shalt thou go, and dust shalt thou eat all the days of thy life."

DEDICATORY EPISTLE

91. Swinburne's "best and dearest friend" was Theodore Watts-Dunton, originally Theodore Watts (1832–1914), to whom he dedicated the collected edition of his poems.

91. Thirty-six years. The American edition, issued in 1905, reads "thirty-eight years." Cf. p. 13.

92. My notes then taken. *Notes on Poems and Reviews.*

93. The fundamental and final principle of union. Swinburne is thinking of his position on the Irish question—a point also discussed in his "Changes of Aspect" (first published in *PMLA* for March, 1943, by the editor of this book; included in *New Writings by Swinburne,* edited by Cecil Y. Lang).

94. My first book. *The Queen-Mother and Rosamond* (1860).

94. The authors of "Tamburlaine the Great," "King Henry VI.," and "Sir Thomas Wyatt" were respectively Marlowe, Shakespeare, and Webster.

95. "Occuper . . . vous." "To occupy these two summits is uniquely your privilege," Hugo wrote to Swinburne.

95. Sir Henry Taylor (1800–1886), as the author of *Philip van Artevelde,* seemed to Swinburne an especially good judge.

96. *Caractacus* was the work of William Mason (1724–1797) and *Merope* that of Matthew Arnold.

99. From Ercildoune to Florence. Because of his inheriting land in Ercildoune, or Erceldoune, a Scottish village, an English writer of the thirteenth century to whom a poem on Tristram has been assigned is called Thomas of Erceldoune. Florence is mentioned because of Swinburne's awareness of Dante's familiarity with the story.

99. "A more plausible objection" was made by the *Saturday Review,* LIV (July 29, 1882), 156–57.

100. Theseus . . . Arcite. Chaucer's Knight's Tale, lines 2987 ff.

100. "Four poems of the West Undercliff," describing scenes on the

Isle of Wight, are those mentioned later—"In the Bay," "On the Cliffs," the "Dedication" to *The Sisters,* and "A Forsaken Garden."

101. The very words of Sappho . . . nightingales. In "On the Cliffs."

101. The presence of dead poets. In "In the Bay."

101. The half-brained creature . . . libraries. Swinburne's response to a recurring charge of bookishness.

101. The relics of Dunwich. In "By the North Sea."

102. The splendid oppression . . . nympholepsy. In allusion to "A Nympholept."

103. Philip Sidney is commemorated in "Astrophel." Aurelio Saffi was a friend of Mazzini's whom Swinburne met at Oxford.

103. Tennyson and Browning. Swinburne paid tribute to Tennyson in "Threnody" and to Browning in "A Sequence of Sonnets on the Death of Robert Browning."

103. Bruno inspired "For the Feast of Giordano Bruno" and "The Monument of Giordano Bruno."

103. Matchless succession of poets. In "Sonnets on English Dramatic Poets."

104. The Globe, the Red Bull, or the Black Friars. Elizabethan theaters.

104. Plays or attempts at plays. Byron was the author of *Marino Faliero, Doge of Venice.* The authorship of *The Lamentable Tragedie of Locrine* (1595) is unknown.

104. An English dramatist of all but the highest rank. Swinburne alludes to Middleton's play, *The Witch;* though he was also familiar with D'Avenant's *The Tragedie of Albovine, King of the Lombards,* his chief source was Machiavelli's *Florentine History.*

105. "Les Djinns" is a poem by Victor Hugo.

105. No music in verse . . . malignity. A response to another recurring criticism.

105. Chœrilus or a Coluthus. Chœrilus of Iasos, an epic poet contemporary with Alexander the Great, is mentioned disparagingly in Horace's *Epistles* (II. 1 and 3). Coluthus, a sixth-century epic poet of Egypt, wrote *The Rape of Helen.*

105. Thornton and . . . Tennyson. Robert Thornton (*fl.* 1440) compiled, though he probably did not write, the so-called Thornton Romances. Some Middle English romances use a stanzaic form similar to that of *The Tale of Balen* and Tennyson's "The Lady of Shalott."

Textual Notes

NOTES ON POEMS AND REVIEWS

1. the attacks [these attacks
2. the usual limits [the limits
3. *In the MS this passage follows:* Nor was I willing to bring forward any matter which would concern myself, had not others assumed the right to make it their affair. With equal silence and equal scorn I had hoped to pass by the scurrility of this man and the treachery of that. Others, not I, may be curious to inquire whether a breach of contract were spontaneous or suggested. It is enough for me, on conviction of a man's unworthiness of trust, to decline any further dealing with such an one and withdraw from his hands, on any terms, all property of mine which they had held. Exposure could hardly discredit those who court detection; and the makers and breakers of contracts may be left to fatten on the fruits of their furtive audacity. I pass on to things, however contemptible, yet for the moment of more importance than such as these. I have undertaken to say
4. *Unlike the MS, the first edition uses quotation marks around the quoted lines* (*cf. p. viii, above*). *The MS continues:* But I am told by the publisher who is about to reissue my poems, that he is on that account distinctly threatened with prosecution by persons responsible for the menace, having names of their own and faces not muffled under masks.
5. the wish of my present publisher [his wish
6. by circumstances . . . book *omitted in the MS*
7. what phrase . . . virtue [what phrase can have provoked so strange a menace? what hidden sin can have drawn down such thunder from the serene heavens of public virtue?
8. been impugned by judges, [been e.g. impugned, by judges
9. *After* blasphemous *in the MS:* These somewhat vague terms the judges have not taken trouble to define; these very vague charges they have not taken trouble to prove.
10. *After* the kind *in the MS:* An atheist has as much right to call me a fanatic as a fanatic to call me an atheist; for in no passage of my writings have I professed or indicated an adherence to either side. For proof of this I need only refer to the volume now under debate: in which, according to the mood I wished to represent, I have spoken alternately as the mouthpiece of one and of the other.

I pass now to the charge of "impropriety"; and first of all I have to say that if in any work of mine I could discover anything so scurrilous and obscene as some of the commentaries issued against my last book, I should be the first to tear out, ashamed and repentant, the disgraceful page. But I need not say I have found none such.

11. such unexpected honour. [the unexpected honour?

12. I have never lusted . . . , *occurring in both MS and 1st ed., takes the place of a passage canceled in the MS:* Like Mrs. Jonathan Wild (nee Lætitia Snap), I am altogether out-argued, perplexed, and beaten out of sight or speech; I can only articulate—"But methinks, Mr. Wild, I would fain know why——?" And after a few minutes' reflection I do know—or conjecture. Virtue is an abyss, and fetid odours rise out of it; (I speak now of the "virtue" incarnate in British journalism, and voluble through that unsavoury outlet;)

13. *The MS thus continues:* To others I have only to say this; What is it that these nameless (and unmentionable) persons find assailable or objectionable in these verses of mine? I for one cannot conceive. They talk of something "foul," of something "unspeakable." What is it? They refuse to explain. I challenge them to the proof; but the answer, I fear, will be silence or evasion. For in this poem

14. poets both [poets, they

15. at sight of her favourite by the side [at the sight of her female favourite in the arms

16. And if to [If to

17. an offence [an indictable offence

18. its publishers—Messrs. Moxon and Co. [the publishers—Messieurs Moxon and Company, of Dover Street.

19. striven here [tried here

20. for awhile *in both 1st ed. and MS*

21. and doubtful emotions— [and perverse emotions;

22. the spirit, [and the spirit

23. huntress [temptress

24. simple enough; [simple enough:

25. *Tannhaüser in both 1st ed. and MS*

26. a dead art; buried [a dead art, buried

27. fancy; [fancy:

28. evil [vile

29. this tribute [that tribute

30. all men should praise [all men praise

31. all men should scorn [all men scorn

32. fashion [favour

33. *In the MS no new paragraph follows the quotation*

34. the stream and somewhat cold [the stream, somewhat cold

UNDER THE MICROSCOPE

1. all study [the study
2. other parasites [other (polypodal) parasites
3. by any fair means [by any means
4. not expect [not hope (hope *replaces* expect, *marked out*)
5. it be [it is
6. I imagine [Imagine
7. a new-comer [an intruder
8. her colleagues; [her collegians;
9. Would it be [Would he find it
10. men; bring [men, bring
11. in preference [by preference
12. same subject. [same subject:
13. second-hand [second hand
14. monsieurs [messieurs
15. the German biographer, [the German biographer
16. gunpowder, and Milton's [gunpowder and Milton's
17. just this; [just this,
18. noblest examples [noblest samples
19. Clytæmnestra, with [Clytemnæstra with
20. evils ensuing; [evil ensuing;
21. Agamemnon, [Agamemnon
22. Clytæmnestra [Clytemnæstra
23. depress the design [deform the design
24. drama, [drama
25. story, by [story by
26. dignity; [dignity:
27. more or less symbolic agents and patients which [strumpets and scoundrels, broken by here and there an imbecile, which
28. *said Vivien,* [said Vivien,
29. changeless change; [changeless change:
30. the one thing needful; [the one thing needful,
31. do this thing or to be that thing [be this thing or to do that thing
32. second-hand [second hand
33. has ever done; [has ever done,
34. The present poets of Greece, [Its present poets,
35. Feudalism in [Feudalism, in
36. We have *in the MS does not introduce a new paragraph*
37. head-masters [headmasters
38. for awhile *in both 1st ed. and MS*
39. pejor; [pejor:

40. from our own.* [from ours.*
41. to pieces, [to pieces
42. describes [described
43. Πολλòs, *in both MS and 1st ed. the first word of the Greek lines, was listed among the errata. In the MS, the last word has an acute rather than the grave accent of the 1st ed.*
44. ταῦτον [ταὐτòν
45. In effect *does not begin a new paragraph of the MS*
46. the critic, who [the critic who
47. contemporary however [contemporary, however,
48. aim unprovoked at [aim at
49. beasts of game; [beasts of game:
50. *The 1st ed. has a half-stop after the Greek quotation. The MS has a period, beginning a new sentence with* From
51. merely repulsive; [merely repulsive—
52. street-walker, as [street-walker as
53. "gallows-carrion;" is ["gallows-carrion"—is
54. taken into [*originally* touched upon with
55. Hugos . . . Brownings [Hugo's . . . Browning's
56. journals, must [journals must
57. same subject; who would admit [same subject, and admit
58. handling, which (handling which
59. his patron; [his patron:
60. *The MS thus continues the paragraph:* Less pardonable however would it be even in a scribbler as low in rank as this, if it were proved that his malignity had been elicited while his cowardice was alarmed by the conscience of recent plagiarism, by the remembrance of anything stolen by anticipation from the yet unpublished 'Drama of Kings' to cover the nakedness of 'Songs before Sunrise'; a theft as unparalleled as this would surely be since Byron and Scott stole some of their best-known images (also by anticipation) from the yet unpublished pages of Robert Montgomery; as may be seen by a reference to Macaulay's Essays. In both cases, however, if there were really anything of petty larceny in the matter, it must be allowed that the articles filched were hardly recognizable when set forth on the counter of the thief.
61. denied us; [denied us:
62. inadvertence ['inadvertence'
63. contemporary ['contemporary'
64. *The MS has* Grubstreet (*not hyphenated*); *in the 1st ed.* Grub-*comes at the end of a line (in Swinburne's day, three spellings were possible)*

Index

Since Swinburne often quotes or alludes to authors without identifying them, the index cites relevant pages in the explanatory notes. Such page references are italicized.

Newgate, 84 n.
Newton, Sir Isaac, 55
Niobe, 28
Non(n)otte, Claude-François, 86, *124*

Offenbach, Jacques, 54
Oldmixon, John, 45, *112*
Orestes, 72
Origen, 23, *108*
Orton, Arthur. *See* "Tichborne claimant, the"
Otho, King of Greece, 65 n.

Pantaloon, 38
Patmore, Coventry, *109*
Pentecost, 52, *113*
Pericles, 65 n.
Petronius: Buchanan on, 61, 73, 84, *123*
Philips ("Phillips"), Ambrose, 20, *107*
Pindar, 65 n., 97
Plato, 28, *108*
Poe, Edgar Allan, 67
Pontmartin, A. M. de, 37, *110*
Pope, Alexander: quoted, 36, *110;* Byron's ranking of, 54; as a formalist comparable to Whitman, 62; mentioned, 44
Porson, Richard, 76, *120*
Porter, Noah, 1
Priapus, 42, *119*
Punch, 5, 9

Quarterly Review, the, 38–39, 42–43, *110, 111*

Rochester, Lord, 55
Roscommon, Earl of, 77
Rossetti, Christina, 103
Rossetti, Dante Gabriel: Buchanan's attack on, 7; ignorance of Buchanan's writings, 73, 75, *119;* "Jenny," *119*
Rossetti, William Michael: discusses Swinburne's defense, 2; reference to Buchanan, 6; labors for, and faith in, Whitman, 10, 62; letter to, *107*
Ruskin, John, 70, *118*
Rymer, Thomas, 86, *124*

Saffi, Aurelio, 103, *126*
Saintsbury, George, 5

Sappho: odes, 20, 97; use of her words in a poem, 101, *126*
Saturday Review, the: Morley's attack on *Poems and Ballads,* 1, 28, *109;* criticism of *Songs before Sunrise,* 3, *113,* and of *Tristram of Lyonesse,* 99, *125*
Scott, Sir Walter: edition of Dryden, 50; his Major Dalgetty, 61, *115*
Settle, Elkanah, 50
Shakespeare, William: quoted or adapted, 22, 43, 44, 48–49, 54, 55, 57, *107, 111, 112, 114;* compared by Byron with Pope, 54; his Cleopatra, 60; point of view in *Coriolanus,* 66, and other plays, 66–67; Doll Tearsheet, 72; Buchanan on, 73, *120;* facts of his life hidden, 75; mentioned, 53
—*As You Like It,* 87, *124; Hamlet,* 55, 56, 77, *121; Henry VIII,* 85, *124; King Henry VI,* 94; *King Lear,* 54, 104, *114; Merry Wives of Windsor,* 57, *114; Midsummer-Night's Dream,* 87, *125; Othello,* 56, 104; *Pericles,* 44, *112*
Shelley, Percy Bysshe: iconoclasm, 18, 22 n.; quoted, 19, 22 n., 27, 50, *107, 113;* interest in Hermaphroditus, 27–28 n.; his lyric power compared with Byron's, 54; lines on the death of Napoleon, 56; song of the earth from *Prometheus Unbound,* 65 n.; Buchanan on, 73, *120;* concern with poor, 79, *121;* mentioned, 53, 82 n., 85, 96, 100, 105
Sheridan, R. B.: his Joseph Surface, 82, *122*
Sidney, Sir Philip: his precept, 92; tribute to, 103, *126*
Simonides, 28
Sophocles: story of Oedipus, 54, *115*
Spectator, the: reviewer in, cited, 68, 69, *117*
Stowe, Harriet Beecher: article on Byron, 9; discussed, 51–52, *113*
Strahan and Company, 8
Stuart, Mary, 27
Swinburne, Algernon Charles: algolagnia, 4; hoaxes, 12; invective, 11–12;